COMPARATIVE POLITICS AND CRISIS OF GOVERNANCE:
THE RUSSIAN CONUNDRUM

COMPARATIVE POLITICS AND CRISIS OF GOVERNANCE:
THE RUSSIAN CONUNDRUM

Dr Sudhir Kumar

Vij Books India Pvt Ltd
New Delhi, India

Published by

Vij Books India Pvt Ltd
2/19, Ansari Road, Darya Ganj
New Delhi - 110002
Phones: 91-11-65449971, 91-11- 43596460
Fax: 91-11-47340674
e-mail : vijbooks@rediffmail.com
web : www.vijbooks.com

First Published : 2011

ISBN 13 : 978-93-80177-66-3

TABLE OF CONTENTS

LIST OF TABLES AND FIGURES

Tables

Figures

FOREWORD

Across the world the first decade of the twenty first century has begun with the people's demands for a participatory , accountable and democratic government that ensures human rights. The idea that governments must respond to these demands has led to new revolutions, even in areas and cultures that were tightly controlled by military dictatorships and dynasties.

The democratic revolution ushered in by the Russian people in 1991 and end of decades of authoritarian rule of the Communist Party of the Soviet Union was the beginning of a new wave of such revolutions. This change was meant to bring a level of free market, democracy and individual rights. What we witnessed in the early decade of this change that followed the breakup of Soviet style institutions was the promotion of a free reign of markets and the creation of formal institutions that were to democratize the political system. The Russian Constitution (brought in through a non democratic framework) proclaimed a presidential system, features of parliamentary democracyfederal regioanlsim and rule of law . Elections to these bodies have followed on a regular basis.

But critical questions are being raised about the Russian political system. Is Russia giving its people the kind of government they wanted in place of the old authoritarian one? Do Russian people have a share in the new sovereignty? Do they have rights and a liberal framework that the Constitution promised? Are they able to live with dignity? Or that a new oligarchic capitalism based on client patron and crony relations with formalistic institutions has taken the place of the old structures signifying a distortion of the idea of democracy?

One way of measuring the legitimacy and performance of governments is by analyzing governance and public policy . This appraisal can judge the ability of governments to implement their mandate and if not what are the reasons for this failure. The caveat here also is whether elected regimes are serious about governance and policy implementation, as opposed to perpetuating their power through other means. Literature on the Russian political system that focuses on problem of law and order , violation of constitutional law or corruption as outcomes of failure of democratization has emerged in the recent past. This book is unusual in its approach and comparative framework.

This study makes the argument that Russia' s problems should be seen as challenges of making a state that is based on an equal and just society and protecting human rights. The idea of liberal democracy being able to deliver rights in the absence of participatory politics and equity is questioned and many popular theories of comparative politics are also challenged. This book theorizes democratization as the process of building such a state, and not the regime. In addition this study argues that the creation of such a democratic state is not possible without the implementation of democratic governance at every level and in every institution.

Democratic Governance is measured with the criterion of participation, transparency and accountability . The number of cases of violation of constitutional norms, increasing crime rate, large number of polity failures are viewed to show the emergence of a small elite that controls state power and appropriates privileges in the name of democracy   . Russia faces a democratic deficit on account of corruption, crime, unfair elections, and centralization, in addition to controls over press and media. These issues are not difficult to tackle if the regime in power has the political will and the governing elite is convinced that good governance will be in public good.

This book shows how the lack of peoples' participation in the functioning of institutions has negatively impacted policies. It has led to centralization of the political and federal system and encouraged bureaucratization and the re-creation of the nomenklatura, the very reason for the Soviet collapse.

The usefulness of this work lies in the comparative analysis of different countries undergoing political transition especially the post-colonial (e.g. India, South Africa, Pakistan etc.) and post-Soviet cases (e.g. Uzbekistan, Kygyzstan, Ukraine etc.). This is indeed a useful approach as it looks at multi-causal factors of state functioning in transitional societies. Further the measurement of policy outcomes from the point of human development makes this work a valuable addition to the study democracies and how they should function and to say the least how a regime can survive rather than face the wrath of its own people.

-ANURADHA M. CHENOY

PREFACE AND ACKNOWLEDGEMENTS

It was my MPhil dissertation on political parties and party system in Russia which generated a sense of dissatisfaction for the studies of formal 'political institutions and procedures.' In my quest for an alternative I found the idea of governance fascinating as it was more grounded, people centric and above all outcomes based instead of merely analyzing few institutions which were almost predecided in nature. Though there were criticisms against the World Bank notion of governance, the contemporary approaches has learnt a lot from these criticisms and improved accordingly .

The studies in transitiology – study of countries undergoing political and economic change, also switching over from one type of system to another , also suffered from the problems of formal analysis. Focus of these studies was on democracy building where democracy was defined more in the Western sense or how American scholars understood it. Here democratization was defined in a narrow sense, usually in the sense of Robert Dahl's definition of democracy. Multi party system was considered as the most significant pillar of democracy building. They focused more on the Western centered conceptions of institutions or political procedures. In fact, the whole idea of political was also defined in the western sense as leftwitch did in his book on defining the meanings of political it self.

Besides, within India there have been dissatisfied voices against the western way of defining and evolving the whole political structure and procedures. While working in an environment a scholar always gets influenced from such ideas. My quest for difference was also perhaps a part of this environment.

My thanks are due to a number of people who helped me in various ways with the writing of this book. Firstly I am grateful to Dr Sanjay Pandey for his academic and personal support. It was his idea of comparing federal systems especially India and Russia which generated interest for comparative politics. Besides, what have led to reformulation of the idea of democratization were our discussions regarding the rationale behind such comparisons. He has not only been a teacher but also a close friend.   Apart from academic assistance he was always ready with his moral support which helped in continuing this work. In all my difficult moments when I was emotionally weak or financially instable he offered me all possible help going out of way.

Professor Anuradha Chenoy deserves special thanks for multiple reasons. I express my sincere gratitude to her as she agreed to write a foreword for this book. While doing my course *Politics and Society in Post-Soviet Russia* there were interesting and interest generating discussions in the classroom with Prof Anuradha. The analysis of Russian case in this book is an outcome of those discussions.

Besides, it was kind financial assistance of the School of International Studies during my PhD which facilitated my field work in Russia. Perhaps the idea of how states are different in theory and practice, and how does it lead to 'democratic deficit' would have never been possible without my visit to Russia. The help offered by the Carnegie Centre for International Peace, Moscow centre and my friends Peter and   Vika which made my field work possible was invaluable. Besides, the help offered by faculties and students especially Roma, of the Centre for Asian and African Studies, the Moscow State University, Moscow, was of immense help.

The existing theories of state do not really focus on the governance aspect. The popular theories emphasize more on the sociological and economic aspects and less on the political. In political science there are attempts to define political in a restricted and narrow sense – the way economists define economy and sociologists explain sociology But is it really possible to separate political from the economy and society? It was this question which made me to study state from the governance perspective where the focus should be on all aspects of society which affect a collective decision making.

My sincere thanks to Dr. Amit Prakash who actually explained me what governance is all about. Being a student of Area Studies it was my limitation to study governance and state issues from the perspective of comparative politics. It was his guidance that I could work on this area. He was also a motivational force behind my critical understanding for the ideas which we usually accept the way there are in the books. He always asked –why this? The same question I am trying to pose in this book. Is there only one way of looking democracy? I am also thankful to the examiners of my PhD thesis whose value able comments helped me in improving the thesis.

I am also thankful to my former supervisor Professor Nirmala Joshi who has always been very supportive and encouraging. In fact it was her guidance that I could think of selecting a different and challenging area of investigation. She always stood by me whenever I called her for any assistance. I am extremely thankful to Dr. Rajan Kumar for his valuable suggestions on the theoretical aspects of democratization and research model. Dr. Rajan's friendly nature was always a source of inspiration for me. It was his company which has motivated me to choose academics as a profession. Dr. Arun Mohanty helped me in the sections on Russian bureaucracy and economic revival. I heavily relied upon their expertise on these areas.

Various chapters were read and commented by my other colleagues in the Centre for Russian and CentralAsian Studies. I am also thankful to Professor Ajay Patnaik, Professor Tulsi Ram, Dr. Gulshan Sachdeva and Dr. Phool Badan. I also express my thanks to friends Govind Kumar Inakhiya, Sidhartha Mukherji, Brajesh, Dr. Shashi Kant Pandey, Dr. Ripusudan Singh and Jaya Srivastava and Shefalika who have been there with me in all times. I was also supported by my classmates Saroj Rani and Shradha during this work.

I was always helped by the office staff members of the Centre for Russian and Central Asian Studies especially Mr. M.M. Handa, Vijay and Gurpreet. They took care of all my documents related formalities without taking much time. It would have not been possible for me to complete this thesis without their support. The JNU central library staff was also very kind in providing all necessary journals and books. The resources in the Nehru Memorial Library, British Council Library, and American Cultural Central Library were other sources of information.

No academic study can be completed without a congenial climate at home. My parents have always been supportive whenever it came to the issue of academic work. They have also relieved me from certain responsibilities back home even at times when it was essential.

Above all it was Shailza's efforts which always motivated me to complete the task of converting my PhD dissertation into a book. She always persuaded me to update my understanding of Russia and theories of comparative politics. During tough moments she always stood by me. She not only kept her expectations aside whenever I was busy with the book, but took so many additional burdens despite having so many additional responsibilities. In fact she is the one who has suffered the most during this work but it was her smile which made me to work harder for the manuscript.

In the end I thank Brigadier PK Vij, managing director of Vij Books India Pvt Ltd who had been very cooperative and tolerant. He has tolerated my habit of missing the deadlines. Above all there were many others whose name cannot be mentioned here because of paucity of space deserves special thanks. I take full responsibility for all the mistakes in the book, which certainly will be there.

- Author

Introduction

Whither Comparative Politics

This study is an attempt to explain the political changes taking place in the post-Soviet states and Russia in particular.While focusing on the emergence and nature of the state it tries to explain the political developments with the help of governance related variables.The study argues that non participatory, non transparent and unaccountable governance has resulted into emergence of a centralized, corrupt and weak Russian state. Emergence of such state has negatively affected the ongoing process of democratization. Besides, the study critically analyses the existing methods of comparative politics for explaining such changes and suggests an alternative approach called governance approach. The study argues that the modern literature on comparative politics suffers from twofold problems. Firstly, it attempts to promote the western model as ideal and secondly it emphasizes more on similarity of the cases for comparison rather than looking for the cases which are different in nature. Specifically, the literature looking into the ongoing political and economic changes in the post-Soviet space has been focusing more such problems.

Evolution of Comparative Politics

The development of literature in comparative politics can broadly be divided into three phases (Beyme 2008). [1] The first phase, called as the pre-modern literature begins withAristotle till the emergence of modernity in the twentieth century. This phase was characterized by its focus on the similarity of the cases. The second phase was of classical modernists, which begins from

---

[1] It is important here to clarify that this section attempts to provide a critique of the existing comparative politics literature and not of the methodology of comparative politics. Methods can always be used for certain predefined objectives. For more discussion on the issue how political influences comparative politics see Beyme 2008: 40-41.

scholars like MaxWeber, Hegel, Marx, Mill and so on and goes till the emergence of post-modernity. The modern phase was full of diver gent views on the nature and methods of comparisons in social sciences. Besides, by the end of the twentieth century the focus of comparative politics been shifted from comparative politics to comparing policies. The post-modern comparative politics literature is characterized by 'variables' i.e. 'comparative aspects have to be kept variables' (Caramani 2008: 28-42).

The Critique

Despite various 'waves' of comparative sciences, an overview of the literature shows that there are certain trends which continue to remain dominant in the comparative analysis till date. Firstly, similarity of cases is a criteria behind selection of the cases and secondly the western models [2] continue to be portrayed as ideals.Although the discipline of comparative politics has travelled a long way in terms of methodology but the existing research has not been able to come up with a more fruitful and neutral research.

Although John Stuart Mill criticized the pre-modern comparative analysis for its over emphasis on 'similarities' of the cases, but even the modern literature of comparative politics continues to suffer from this problem (Mill 2002). Despite various claims that the comparative methods are also based upon the Most Different Systems Design (MDSD), the truth of comparative politics is that similarities are still the primary criteria behind selection of cases. The problems which are taken up for investigation are more from the perspective of western type political systems most of the time. The analysis is more like an attempt to fit the problems of developing societies into the western world paradigms that is to say, it is nor problem orriented from the perspective of the non-west.

This criticism can well be explained with the analysis on the democratization literature. In fact a larger chunk of literature in comparative politics has been centered on the issues of democracy building or consolidation.

---

[2] The term Western model is used here for the countries which are considered as developed such as US, UK and so on. The popular western models are taken from these two coun-tries.

In fact, the most influential and popular writings of comparative politics are on democracy only . Though these studies have greatly contributed to the global understanding of politics, democracy and development but they have failed to incorporate the non-western models of development.

This phenomenon has resulted into glorifying or eulogizing the western models at any cost and criticizing the non-western models on the similar criteria. For instance, the western democracies have been suffering more from the problem of regional inequality, crime and so on. But the focus area of research in comparative politics has been the success stories of western democracies and institutionalism and not their shortcomings (Huntington 1968; Dahl 1956, 2000; Linz *et al* 1996). However, most of the literature on comparative studies suffers from the problem of narrowness in their scope.

The similar criticisms can also be seen in the literature on the World Bank approach to governance and liberal theory which came up in the 1990s (Jayal 1997; Guhan 1998). The governance approach was criticized for picking up the questions which were more to defend the agenda of developed economy, especially the market, instead of really looking into the problems which were being faced by the poorly governed countries.

Similarly, the comparative politics literature has failed to develop set of research questions which are more inclined towards addressing a problem which is cross-country in nature. Rather, only the similar kinds of questions are being taken up for investigation.

The problem with the comparative politics literature in general and democratization studies in particular is their narrow approach. The selections in the comparative studies are based on the notion that some similarities should exist between the cases which are being compared. The most important commonality which the comparativists seek is the cultural similarity of the cases. It is assumed that similarity of culture leads to similar problems and therefore there can be uniform mechanisms to study such examples. [3] For

---

[3] For more on this issue see Gabriel Almond's article, "The Development of Political Development" in Myr on Weiner and Samuel P . Huntington (1987), eds. *Understanding Political Development* (Boston: Little, Brown and Co.), pp. 437-490.

example, the popular study on democratization and authoritarianism in Latin America by O'Donnel and J. Scheimtter focuses exclusively on the Latin American region or on the post-Communist Europe.

These similarities have become so important a criteria that the real objective of comparison is being ignored. In the recent past the discipline of comparative politics has become a discipline of analyzing only one dominant question i.e. how democratization is taking place.All other question focusing in the discipline are by and large focusing only on related questions such as what helps in enduring authoritarianism, what hampers democracy building, what is the nature of various political institutions and so on. In other words, the concern has been either the west or the west type institutions or cultures.

In addition to this there has been a widespread tendency to define political processes and institutions in terms of being 'political.' Political here is evolution of certain institutions and the values and norms of them in the manner they have evolved in the developed countries of the Western Europe or America. For instance, there is a global consensus on how parliaments should function or how market should be incorporated in the decision making and program implementation. Such conclusions are not really based upon the local conditions of the countries for which they are being suggested.   As a result such experiments are failing one by one in many countries.

During 1970s, after facing vehement criticisms from the dependency theorists there was a change in the way research was being conducted in the discipline (Diamond *et al.* 1989). The dependency theorists brought in various issues which were more about the growing regional disparities across the globe. However, the dependency theory could not sustain for long due to various reasons. Especially, the economic issues which were the prime focus in the dependency, gradually were challenged by the emer ging literature on globalization. This led to the decline of dependency theory from the discipline (Leys 1996). Since then the discipline of comparative politics has become extremely 'political' in nature, where the focus is exclusively on political institutions, structures and processes. It tends to ignore many more serious issues emerging in the modern 'post-modern' world.

Do we suggest that there should not be any global understanding over the principles to be followed in the governance? Is this criticism like the post-modernist critique which demands more attention for consideration of local conditions instead of imposing certain pre defined concepts and theories. In fact, in this study it is suggested that what needs to be done is to evolve ways of analysis where issues and not types of institutions and procedures are discussed. For example, the issue of theft deserves serious attention but there cannot and should not the similar ways of addressing this crime in the similar manner across the world. The police system cannot have similar way of handling such crime in New York and Dhaka.

This does not prevent us from the need of developing a global understanding of analyzing various issues. Corruption is a world wide challenge. Crime is a serious problem not only in the developed but also in the developing countries. The present study attempts to argue that in order to make the analysis more issue oriented there is a need to develop a different understanding of democratization. Instead of being defined in terms of certain particular types of institutions or procedures, the need is to explain whether democracy is emerging or not. For this purpose we need to adopt a wider perspective of the problem of democratization.

The objective of comparative politics is to compare various political units in order to understand a political system or many political systems keeping in view one common set of problems. These problems do not necessarily have to be political in nature as in the modern world economic, political and social problems are deeply intertwined. The discipline of comparative politics is also expected to explain how various countries are managing their political affairs. Ironically, the present approaches to comparative politics are focusing more on the similarities and less on the outcomes achieved with the help of such comparisons. Deontology has become the primary concern and not the consequence.[4]

For instance India is compared mostly with its South   Asian neighbors like Pakistan, Nepal, and Bhutan and so on. Only in the last decade

---

[4] For more on the issue of procedure and consequences see Amartya Sen (2009), *Idea of Justice* (Penguine: New Delhi).

comparativists have started comparing the Indian polity with other developed democracies and economies of the world. Only in the recent past attempts have been made to compare Chinese case with the Indian model of economic development.

Similarly, the comparative politics literature in case of post-Soviet countries has largely produced two types of comparisons: one, inter-regional comparisons e.g. comparison between the Central Asia, Eastern Europe, and Transcaucasia etc. (McF Aul 2000, White 2000, Munro 2003, Bunce 2003) and two, cases within a particular region such as comparing Central   Asian states with each other . A third category of comparisons has also emer   ged comparing the post-Soviet states with the countries of Eastern Europe which were not part of the Soviet Union. Such studies are rare in numbers. The transitologists have focused on these states due to the similarities in their culture, political history etc. An ethno-centric bias is clearly visible in case of such comparisons as most of the comparative studies produced in the local language compare only the post-Soviet cases. Western scholars, on the other hand, either compare the post-Soviet examples with each other or with the East European cases. This has been so as some of the countries of the Former Soviet Union are considered close to the European society (Pandey 2007). Similarly, the East European cases are compared with the OECD countries due to their cultural closeness with the Western Europe.

These studies are negligent of the fact that the problems prevailing in the countries can be similar or different irrespective of similar cultures, politics or other factors. [5] For instance India and China are comparable as both are facing the challenge of managing the development of a billion plus population in a high growth economy . Similarly, the US and India are facing similar challenges to their internal security in the form of terrorism. India and Russia are facing similar challenges to their federal polities. India and Sri Lanka are facing challenge of accommodating the demands of ethnic minorities. India and many countries of Africa are facing serious challenge of malnutrition,

---

[5] It is pertinent to mention here that similarity of cases do not mean identical cases. Even the existing studies do not see identity amongst the cases taken for analysis but only few similarities. However, these very basis of similarit y are questioned here.

higher infant mortality rates etc. Similarly Russia and Japan are facing serious demographic challenge. Taking these problems into account there is a need to develop an approach to comparative politics where the focus is on the problem and how different states have been dealing with these problems. [6]

One such crucial issue which has been affecting democratization, governance and state-building in the countries undergoing economic transition is the rising income and regional inequalities. Although various studies have made serious attempts to look into these challenges but the focus area has been the developed countries, especially the US, Western Europe etc or some developing countries like China, India or Brazil. Many significant regions like the post-Communist regions have not received much attention in this respect.

Though in the recent past, especially after the emergence of post-modern literature, there are attempts to address these questions in an adequate manner However, a larger focus continues to remain on the issues which were dominant during the mid to end of the twentieth century . There is a need to address questions which are trans-regional in nature.

Democratization here is defined as a *process of achieving social equality and justice in a society*. Only through such a process *the demos* will have a collective decision making for themselves. This definition leaves the methods of achieving such equality open. There cannot be a universally similar method. However, in order to achieve such a status there is a need to have people's participation in the decision making at the social level. The social level here could be a state centered organization, regional organization or global organization. The next crucial question needs to be asked –how to make a system more participatory. This demands transparency and accountability or fairness in public affairs. This can be achieved with an effective parliament or a strong presidency as well. The world has shown how British parliament and US presidency have helped in developing a fair system.

---

[6] In a recent study Vernani has made an attempt to compare various countries on the bases of their human development and other challenges irrespective of their culture and political systems.

The question

After looking into the problems with the existing approaches in comparative politics are facing the question which is being discussed in this study is: how to study the emerging problems in the polities undergoing transition while keeping the above mentioned problems away . For this purpose, this study attempts to study the problems of transition in general and challenges coming up in Russia in particular . The study takes up the variables which are not common for the literature in comparative politics. Besides, this study also incorporates examples from the transition in the post-colonial phase in order to provide a more holistic understanding of transition, democratisation and governance.

The study argues that the analysis of nature of the state can be more useful for democratization analysis than the popular approaches which keep issues like elections, constitution in theory, and political institutions, at their center. It can also be more helpful in explaining how far the political system is distributive and participatory in its nature. I further argue that the governance approach, that takes into account the implementation of the application of certain principles like: participation, transparency and accountability can better explain the nature of state. Such an approach is more useful in explaining the problems of transitional political societies in general and Russia in particular

The argument

The focus of the studies on democratization and transition polities has been more on certain popular areas of political science e.g. institution building, procedures etc. Here the study looks at certain outcomes which are not seen as directly related to political transition. Crisis of Governance is a crucial challenge to democratization. Here crisis of governance means the increasing number of cases of violation of constitutional norms, increasing crime rate, large number of polity failures and so on. The study attempts to show how lack of effective participation, transparency and accountability has led to emergence of a state which is limited in its scope, ineffective in implemented its own policies and above all being run by a small section of elite called the oligarchs. In other words, the undemocratic governance has led to creation of an ineffective state in the post-Soviet Russia.

Organization of the book

The book is structured on the basis of above mentioned argument. Beginning with the theoretical explanation and looking at the existing literature critically the first chapter deals with the theories of state and democratization. Here it is shown how the concept of governance can be used for explaining state capacity. The 'governance approach' is based on the assumption that commonly accepted principles of democratic-governance, such as participation, transparency and accountability , are better parameters for understanding state efficiency and effectiveness, which are further important determinants of democratisation.

Second chapter explains the challenges of state building in the post-Soviet Russia. It also looks into the challenges of governance after the collapse of soviet state. How growing crime has af   fected the state' s ability to governance. How lower participation has affected the decision making in an effective manner.

The third chapter discusses issues of participation in the post-Soviet Russia. It analyses elections and voters turn out. It also explains how the issue of participation was ignored since the beginning of transition, i.e. the beginning of constitution making. Even till date democratic governance is missing from the election process. As a result elections have failed to emerge as genuine mechanisms to raise people's issues. Rather the state itself decides the outcome of elections.

Next chapter looks into the of political institutions like the parliament, the political parties and civil society groups in making the state accountable and their failure in ensuring it due to the concentration of power in the hands of the presidency. As a result the presidency has a free hand in policy making which has resulted in a centralized state structure.

Chapter five shows the outcomes of absence of principles of democratic governance. It shows how these tendencies have resulted into an elite centric state in the post-Soviet Russia. This has further resulted into opposition against the state amongst the deprived sections, and in the poor regions. It shows how growing crime, regional inequality and constitutional violation etc., defined as 'catastrophic governability', are the natural outcomes of such practices.

Chapter six analyses the issue of corruption across the Russian federation. In order to favor few sections corruption has been a strong practice in the post-Soviet Russia. Absence of mechanisms to ensure transparency in various public matters and weakness of public institutions to keep a check on such tendencies has resulted into declining tax revenue. This has also led to decline in people's faith in the political and administrative institutions of the country.

Finally, The concluding chapter deals with the lessons to be leant in comparative politics from the analysis of Russian case. It also dwells upon the possibilities of future research in the governance approach.

Chapter 1

Theorizing Political Transition:
Rebringing The State Via Governance Approach

The global financial crisis has reinforced role of the state in bringing sustained economic stability and effective political control. But the transition literature has not paid adequate attention to the question of building an 'inclusive, capable and efficient state' in the post-Soviet states in general and Russia in particular A major reason behind this is the lack of an acceptable approach to state which can bring democracy and state capacity together. In fact, the question that who controls the state in reality remains almost untouched. Whatever the existing work is, its about the dominance of few on the economy .

However, most of the studies on the politics of these countries have not looked into the nature of political control. In case of Central Asian states the tendency of promoting the family members by the ruling personality is still a generalized fact. But in case of Russia no such explanations are available. This question deserves serious attention as all policies are being made in the name of people's welfare, participation and so on. Former President Boris Yeltsin nominated his Prime Minister Vladimir Putin as his successor. People overwhelmingly supported him. Just before completion of his second tenure Putin declared Dmetri Medvedev as his choice for presidential post. Medvedev won over others. In other words, politics in the post-Soviet Russia is nothing but a 'one man' show – the president. An analysis of Russian political system shows how a coalition of industrialists, mafia, bureaucrats and politicians are governing the new Russian state. Though in theory the rule of law exists but its features are being decided by this coalition. All other institutions such as elections, parties, civil society organizations and media are being managed so beautifully that they exist but do not work.

In reality, rampant corruption and growing crime are the dominant phenomena. The political transition theories do not focus on this sociological analysis of emerging states in the post-Soviet states. In fact, even in case of post-Colonial states this was realized quite late. The state-in-society approach can be helpful in this regard. However, the next crucial question arises – how to explain the nature of emerging states.

The proposed governance approach can be extremely useful in explaining the emerging policy, economy and above all the changing dynamics of the state-society relations. Such an approach incorporates various aspects of democratization: procedural as well as institutional. It also takes into account the real outcomes of such procedures and institutions. Besides, this approach also attempts to raise the question – who governs.

What makes Russian state a perfect case for analysis is the emerging paradox – participatory and competitive democracy in theory but a centralized, non participatory governance system in practice. The erosion of its authority and legitimacy is an outcome of this paradox because it is a certain elite which rule Russia and the state resources are being used for this section. The life of a larger population remains almost unchanged even after almost two decades of so called market reform and democracy building. The governance approach can be used to explain such contradictory tendencies in a state.

I

REBRINGING THE STATE :

In the third century B.C., the famous Greek philosopher Aristotle (384-322 B.C.) regarded state as the highest form of political union, as it represents the pinnacle of social evolution.According to him "an individual found fulfillment from the advantages made possible by the state through its common endeavors, and one who did not feel its need was either an 'angebr a 'beast'" (Mukherjee and Ramaswamy 2004: 105). For   Aristotle state was the most important human organization. Since then the institution of state has remained at the core of various ideologies, controversies and theories.

However, various ambiguities related to the concept of state have made its analysis complicated.[1] Though there have been large number of attempts to explain the concept of state, with the continuously changing socio-political conditions it has been undergoing regular changes. The first such modern attempt was by the German Philosopher Max Weber. According to Weber, "the state is a human community that claims the monopoly of the legitimate use of physical force within a given territory" (Weber 1896). According to this notion what makes state superior as compared to other social organizations is its ability to use coercive force. This definition was a widely accepted definition of state until very recently. However, with the changing nature of politics and economy new actors started coming in and challenged the state's supreme claim to impose laws and regulations over the people living in a particular territory.

There were three major reasons behind it. First was the emergence of behavioralism in the discipline of political science. Emergence of behavioralism in political science brought usage of quantitative techniques and empirical analysis and abstract entities like state were ignored.[2] Issues like economic development, modernization, type of government etc. were given preference over it. Second reason was the emergence of globalization. This brought many new actors; like civil society, multinational corporations, international economic regimes etc, also challenged the supreme authority of the state over its citizens. Besides, with the emergence of Marxism in world politics the influence of society was given a more prominent place than the state. In order to incorporate these issues many scholars felt the need to relook at the definition of state.

It was only in 1970s with the publication of Samuel P. Huntington's article in World Politics which raised the issue of role of state, governability and government (Huntington 1977).Another boost for state was the publication

---

[1] The state, as Brown (1992: 12-13) argues, "is not a thing, system or subject but a significantly unbounded terrain of powers and techniques, an ensemble of discourses, rules and practices, cohabiting in tension-ridden, often contradictory relation with one another."

[2] In the behavioral studies, as Skocpol writes, "the state was considered to be an old-fashioned concept, associated with dry and dusty legal-formalist studies of nationally particular constitutional principles" (Skocpol 1985: 4).

of an edited volume with the title *Brining the State Back In.* Authors in this volume made an attempt to show how state has a crucial role to play in determining the nature of economic development, brining political change and formulating the foreign policies. They tried to show how state can function in an autonomous fashion irrespective of external as well as internal pressures. Consequently, in the last few decades many new studies on the state have come up (e.g. Tilly 1989; Mann 2000; Migdal 2003) describing various aspects of the state.

Michael Mann defines the state as "(i) a differentiated set of and personal embodying (ii) centrality, in the sense that political relations radiate outwards from a center to cover a (iii) territorially , demarcated area over which it exercises (iv) a monopoly of authoritative binding rule-making backed up by a monopoly of authoritative binding rule-making backed by a monopoly of the means of physical violence."

In the contemporary world the state performs a large number of functions as compared to previous centuries (see table below).

Role of State			
	Addressing Market Failures		**Improving equity**
Minimal functions	**Providing pure public goods** Defense, law and order, property rights and Public Health, Macroeconomic management, building perspectives, Anticipatory and prospective tracking of global economy		**Protecting the poor** Anti-poverty programs Disaster relief
Intermediate functions	**Addressing externatilities** Basic education, environment protections	**Regulating monopoly** Utility regulations, Trust p olicy	**Overcoming imperfect information** Insurance (health life, pensions), Financial Regulations, Consumer protection	**Providing social insurance** Redistributive pensions, family allowances, un employment, Insurance, Direct subsidies
Activist functions	**Coordinating private activity** Fostering markets, cluster initiatives State as an entrepreneur and producer of goods and services		**Redistribution** Asset redistribution

Table 1.1
Source: World Development Report 1997: 27

The most significant issue related with the concept of the state is the nature of state. The debate on the nature of the state deals with the state at two levels; first is the state in the international realm, and second, role of the state in domestic issues. At the international level, the debate over state is related to its foreign policy, its role in various international agencies etc. At the domestic level, on the other hand, the issue of nature of state is related with the issues like who dominates the policy making and implementation processes, how effective is the state in resolving various social, territorial and other disputes, and its ability to bring development and so on. The studies related to domestic ability of the state focus on the state and its interrelationship with various social actors. The better state is able to manage these affairs, more efficient the state is.

However, the first question after this arises, why suddenly discussion about state efficiency? After the decolonization wave emergence of new states in Asia and Africa and their failure in ensuring security , stability and implementing state authority in the territory brought this issue came forward. Initially this issue was seen in correlation with the question of democracy building. However, gradually the international community of social scientists and more specifically political scientists and economists realized that it was not simply the question of failure of democracy . The reason was that there were many contrary examples where even states with the authoritarian set up successfully brought remarkable economic growth and higher development as well. It was accepted that without having a stable, efficient and strong state in place it was difficult to achieve democratization. In other words, the state agenda replaced the democracy agenda on the top. The state was accepted as an essential actor in brining political, economic and social changeWithout a state – with its essential features, like a defined territory, a strong standing army and a court system, there can neither be democracy nor an efficient economy.

In their popular volume of democratization Linz and Stepan has shown how the issue of state building or 'stateness' is an important determinant of societies undergoing transition. Similarly, O'Donnell and P. Schmitter have recognized the state as an important factor of analysisThe World Bank (1997) also accepted that the state has a crucial role to play in brining economic development and providing the market suitable conditions. The report recognized certain essential or primary functions of the state.

The issue of state efficiency further emerged as a field of analysis after the World Bank floated the idea of 'good governance.' In its report on the African countries' failed experiment with the market reforms and structural adjustment programs the Bank concluded that lack of good governance was a major cause behind this failure. Though the World Bank idea was criticized on many accounts, it raised a serious issue.Above all, the issue whether good governance incorporates democracy and state building or its focus is more on market building and creating conditions which suits the market, became an issue of debate in the literature of political science, economics and public administration.

Similarly, limitations of traditional democratization studies prompted many comparative political scientists to understand democracy building from a new perspective. Consequently, new studies came up where state was seen as a better unit of analysis (Stepan 1978, McClintock 1981, Stephens and Stephens 1983). These studies focused on the nature of economic and political change and its impact on states.[3] Most of these studies dwell upon the class character of state, the bureaucratic structure and its ability to change the existing character of the society .[4]

Gradually, the World Bank itself realized that the market cannot flourish in the absence of a state system to protect it. The comparative politics literature also started looking into the issue what makes a state efficient. Peter Evans (1998) argued in his book *Embedded Autonomy* that what makes a state efficient is the fact that how deeply it is rooted in the society. Availability of various institutions in order to ensure participation of various social and economic actors in the state policy making and implementation process leads

---

[3] For a detailed analysis of state collapse in Af rica see Z artman, W. (1995) ed., *Collapsed States: The Disintegration and Restoration of Legitimate Authority* (Boulder, Colo: Lynne Reinner).

[4] See Theda Skocpol, Dietrich Rueschemeyer, and Peter Evan, eds. (1985) *Bringing the State Back In*, Cambridge University Press: New York), Lowi (1978).

to higher state autonomy making it ef ficient. Similarly, Joel Migdal (2002) argued in his book that what makes a state more effective is its ability of political mobilization and brining various social and other actors together in the developmental process.

Despite all these positive aspects about the state analysis there is a serious threat implied into it.The emergence of the EastAsian tigers in world economy in spite of authoritarian or semi-authoritarian regimes has brought the issue of development ahead of democracy . Various scholars on democracy have concluded that higher economic development gradually leads to an open and democratic polity. As a result of these studies the sequence of the three changes was seen as, starting from the issue of state building in terms of settlement of territorial issues and institution building, economic modernization with the help of introduction of market reforms and finally democratization process. This became a popular notion across the word during the last decades of the twentieth century.

In an interesting writing on democratization and state building Thomas Carothers has raised question related to the issue of state building. He argues that many of the democracy promoters have ignored the issue of state building. Though state building is not a substitute of democratization, a capable state is essential for developing a smooth democratization.[5]

A capable state cannot be achieved without application of principles of democratic governance. Even if the process of building a capable state begins with an 'autocratic opening' there are always threats to its sustainability.[6]

---

[5] He also discusses the argument that a till the time a strong state is developed, democratization can be kept on hold. See Thomas Carothers (2007), "How Democracies Emerge: The "Sequencing" Fallacy", *Journal of Democracy,* Vol. 18, No. 1, January 2007. However, focus on the strong and effective state and criticizing democratization theories does not mean reversing the sequence. Rather, here it is argued that the an efficient state cannot be achieved without having democratic governance in practice.

[6] Joel Migdal argues that such state cannot sustain in the second phase of state-building. The second phase indicates building rule of law and an effective bureaucratic set up for its implementation. See Joel Migdal (1988), *Strong Societies and Weak States: State Society Relations and State Capabilities in the Third World* (Princeton University Press: Princeton).

The case of Post-Soviet S tates

With the disintegration of the Soviet Union, the leaders of post-Soviet states also decided to follow the popular path of transition. Priority was given to the state-building and economic reforms. Since boundary disputes were not a big issue, the issues at the transition agenda was economic change and the political change. Amongst the two, preference was further given to the latter over the former. In economic change creation of conditions conducive for emergence of the liberal market economy were implemented on the war footingAlthough different countries decided to move with their own pace, economic reforms were almost initiated in all the post-Soviet statesAfter initial phase of economic reforms the political elite also introduced political reforms in the form of western-liberal style of democracy .

For this purpose new constitutions were adopted by all the new states. These constitutional documents were full of the ideas of liberalism, and democracy. Various provisions related to individual rights, civil liberties and freedoms etc. were incorporated and political plurality was also guaranteed with introduction of the multi party system.Territorially bigger and culturally diverse societies like Russia also adopted federal system in order to incorporate demands of various regions. Similarly other provisions were also made to fulfill the demands of the unsatisfied sections.

The issue of state building in this whole process was seen association with the implementation of economic and political reforms. In case of the post-Soviet states, the issue of state-building or stateness in the widely accepted sense, i.e. creating some basic institutions of the state, is not applicable. Unlike other cases, where the process of the state building was to begun from the scratch, in case of these states the legacy of the communist system have provided almost all necessary conditions which are considered as necessary to be recognized as a state. [7] These states have a strong army

[7] Although most of the writings on Russia emphasize on building the Russian state from the beginning but here it is argued that the Russian state has been through many phases of evolution. Presently it is going through a systemic transformation. It fulfills all the conditions which are required for any society to be recognized as a state. Howev er, this is not true in the context of other states which emerged as independent states only after the breakup of the Soviet state. Therefore it is difficult to compare these two types of states in the same category and they demand separate analysis as well.

which has a history of being governed by the civilian government during the Soviet rule. Since the communist ideology gives extraordinary space to the state and bureaucracy these states also have a strong, well established bureaucratic structure. This gave a strong support base to these states. In addition to this, the border disputes are also not as prominent as they have been in case of Asia, like Afghanistan or in Africa like Rwanda and so on. After the collapse of the Soviet state there was no situation of civil war except few examples, like Russia in 1993 and Tajik Civil war. After the collapse of the Soviet state these countries have successfully adopted new constitutions. As a result of these circumstances, the new states did not have the question of building the state from the scratch in the conventional sense.

However, the challenge was quite diferent in nature, i.e. how to establish a more legitimate state with sustainable principles of governance. Despite all these positive situations and modernization experiments, these states especially Russia have been facing problem of governing its population and territory . There have been serous crisis of governability in terms of increasing violence, terrorist activities, growing crime rate, and violation of the federal constitutional provisions. These activities have further led to or have aggravated problems of economic instability and poverty . This has resulted into declining state efficiency in post-Soviet states in general and Russia in particular.

There have not been much focus on the state building in post-Soviet states, at the outset it appears that the case of post-Soviet states especially Russia was seen a peculiar case. The examples of state-building were based on the experience of EastAsia (Evans 1999), West Asia and SouthAsia (Migdal 2001; Kohli 2001). No case of post-Soviet countries was taken into account.

Post-Soviet states are different as they were carrying the features of all other examples. Like West Asia, Russia has all the capabilities to become a rentier state as it has got huge stock of natural resources in the form of oil and gas. Like EastAsian countries Russia has emerged as a country governed by oligarchs.And finally, like SouthAsia countries, especially like India, Russia has a multicultural society with a large territory under its control. Russian has also been facing violent separatist movements on its territory like Kashmir in

South Asia. It also suffers from the problem of increasing crime as India has been facing. All these features make Russian an interesting case of analysis.

In the number of writings which has come up in the recent years only few looks into the problems of state-building in the post-Soviet Russia. The studies on Russian politics and economy seem to be taking the issue of state building for granted or self-explanatory .[8] The studies so far have broadly been focusing on four aspects (see Figure 1.1 below), the elite, the structures, the masses and the agencies. The problem and nature of state-building has not been given adequate attention.

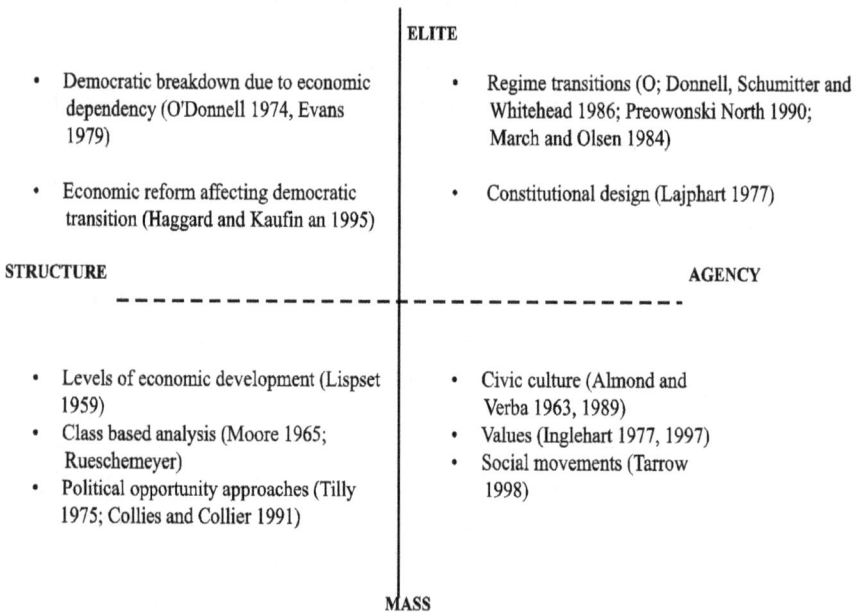

ELITE

- Democratic breakdown due to economic dependency (O'Donnell 1974, Evans 1979)

- Economic reform affecting democratic transition (Haggard and Kaufin an 1995)

- Regime transitions (O; Donnell, Schumitter and Whitehead 1986; Preowonski North 1990; March and Olsen 1984)

- Constitutional design (Lajphart 1977)

STRUCTURE   **AGENCY**

- Levels of economic development (Lispset 1959)
- Class based analysis (Moore 1965; Rueschemeyer)
- Political opportunity approaches (Tilly 1975; Collies and Collier 1991)

- Civic culture (Almond and Verba 1963, 1989)
- Values (Inglehart 1977, 1997)
- Social movements (Tarrow 1998)

MASS

Figure1.1
Different emphasis in the study of the democratization and political transition

---

[8] This criticism has been there for various studies on democracy or economic development in the transitional countries. Scholars on the state argue that the issue of state is considered as self explanatory and ther efore hardly defined categorical ly.

This study argues that these three issues are not separate from each other. However, in order to explain the problem of crisis of governability the concepts which have been taken for granted in the comparative literature such as state, democratization and even democracy need to defined or redefined more categorically (Bunce 2004; Collier and Levitsky 1997; Hyden *et al* 2007).

For instance, in many of the popular writings of democracy in Russia it is even difficult to find one meaning of democratization (Sakwa 1996; MacFaul 2001; White 2001; Neil and Munro 2001). It seems as if the authors assumes the meanings of these phenomena which are perhaps most controversial in the political discourse. Similarly, the meaning of democracy has been modified. Although most of the authors begin with a criticism of the minimalist notion of democracy but they end up following it in some modified framework (Fish 2003). Jean Grugel criticizes democratization studies and their definitions - "these definitions remain quite limited because they fail to take either the issue of power or the importance of structural obstacles to participation seriously" (Grugel 2002: 5). Emphasizing on the need of a broad definition of democratization he further argues – "The litmus test for democracy is not whether rights exist on paper but, rather, whether they have real meaning for the people. Inevitably, this implies a redistribution of power" (Grugel 2002: 6).

In order to explain the practice of democracy this study advocates the analysis of democracy building within the ambit of state building. This will not only explain the democracy on paper and its implications but will also be helpful in investigating whether it brings qualitative change in the power structure. The process of democratization, instead of adopting a minimalist definition, should be defined broadly It should not only incorporate the political institutions and procedures. It should also incorporate output related issues.

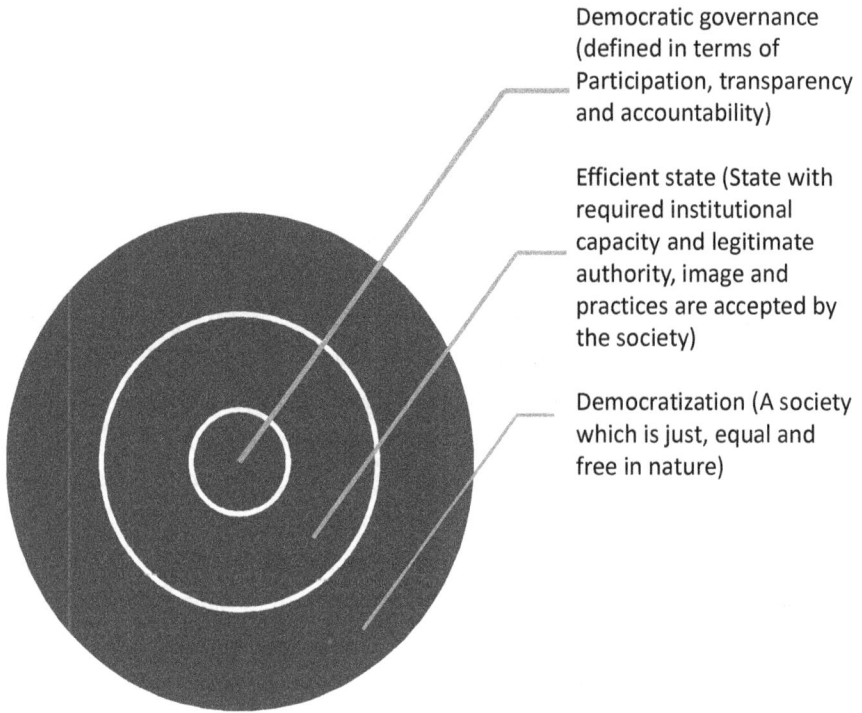

Democratic governance
(defined in terms of
Participation, transparency
and accountability)

Efficient state (State with
required institutional
capacity and legitimate
authority, image and
practices are accepted by
the society)

Democratization (A society
which is just, equal and
free in nature)

Figure 1.2
Governance, democratization and state: An interrelationship

The state-in-society perspective

Similarly, to explain the state capacity in the post-Soviet states there is a need
to adopt a definition of state which not only focuses on institutions and territorial
issues but also looks into its practices as well. For the purpose of this study ,
Joel Migdal's definition of state is taken. Migdal defines a state as "a field of
power marked by the use and threat of violence and shaped by (1) *the image
of a character, controlling organization in a territory, which is a representation
of the people bounded by that territor y,* and (2) *the actual practices of its
multiple parts.*" (Italics in original) (Migdal 2001: 16) The image is described
as: "a dominant, integrated, autonomous entity that controls, in a given territory
all rule making, either directly through its own agencies or indirectly by
sanctioning other authorized organizations – businesses, families, clubs, and
the like – to make certain circumscribed rules." (Migdal 2001: 16). The practices
of a state are defined as "the routine performance of state actors and agencies"

(Migdal 2001: 18). These practices may reinforce the image of the state or weaken it; they may bolster the notion of the territorial and public-private boundaries or neutralize them.

This definition is more appropriate in the modern context compare to some other definitions. Most of the definitions of state emphasize on the state capacity defined in terms of its institutional strength to force its decisions. Migdal's definition on the other hand not only takes into account the institutional capacity of the state defined in terms of 'field of power' but also incorporates modern concerns related to the state i.e. its image and practices. An emphasis on practices is related to the state's ability to govern via public policy while ensuring participation of various social segments. This approach is more helpful in case of countries where in principle the state is based upon liberal democratic values taking into account various issues mentioned in the UN Declaration of Human Rights. However when it comes to practice the state's performance is negative. Instead of protecting the rights of its citizens the state itself has become a threat. Therefore in order to explain the emerging political and other tendencies any definition of state should touch upon the image as well as its practices.

Strong and efficient state

There have been various interpretations of the meaning of strong and weak state. Many scholars equate the strong state with a bureaucratic authoritarian state or a state with strong paraphernalia to force its decisions. For others a strong state is with the capabilities to regulate, to shape eruptive conflicts that emerge due to industrialization or process of modernization or mobilization (Collier 1979; Hewlett and Weinert 1982; Grindle 1977; Frankel 1978; Kohli 1992).

Joel Migdal on the other hand argues that the state is amongst other social organizations where it "seeks predominance over those binding rules guiding people's behavior or, at the very least, to authorize particular social organizations to make those rules in certain realms." (Migdal 2001: 63). Therefore the question of strong-state or weak-state largely depends on "who makes the rules" (Migdal 2001: 64). He further argues that: "Non-compliance is not simply personal deviance or criminality but an indication of a more fundamental conflict over which organizations in society – the state or other organizations – should make these rules." (Migdal 2001: 64).[9]

What makes the case of state building ironic is the behavior of state leaders against the state itself. On the one hand the state leaders try to build various institutions which help them in mobilizing society in their favor   . However, while doing so they also have to ensure their survival.   Therefore they also develop mechanisms which can be further helpful in weakening of the channels created for mobilization purpose. In other words, the state leaders themselves create various state institutions to ensure compliance but at the same time also create anti-state institutions with the help of patronage politics and playing 'dirty tricks' in the administration.

In case of the post-Soviet states, it is interesting to note that though the societies have undergone through radical transformation during the Soviet rule, yet it is struggling with the ideas of building a more effective state. So far the focus has been more on building a strong state defined in terms of its ability to use coercive force, maintaining the territorial integrity and political stability. However, this all has been done at the cost of democratic governance. The modus operandi of the strong state continues to ignore participation, transparency and accountability.

The democratization approaches so far have made attempts to look into the functioning of political systems in Russia.   As discussed earlier , these studies are narrow in their focus as they look into certain political institutions (especially presidency, parliament and political parties). In doing so there conclusions are not very useful while looking at the larger picture of the state. In order to look into micro level issues, this study proposes the governance approach. The governance approach is more holistic and elaborative in nature as it is based upon a large number of indicators. The governance approach here is slightly different from the democratic governance approach followed by the UNDP. The UNDP approach takes into account many variables which

---

[9] Migdal has ar gued that such tendencies ar e rooted into the natur e of societ y. These features are more prominent in the societies which are fragmented in nature, like most of the third world societies are. Therefore the state in these societies continues to be caught in various social conflicts.

can further be incorporated into the three variables identified here as the key governance indicators.

Here the strong state phenomenon is being replaced by the notion of efficient state. An efficient state is defined here as, a state which can enforce its laws on the land on the one hand, and can also ensure the well being of its citizens on the other. A state which is considered as legitimate and right by the society can afford to do so. Unless the state is considered as a genuine organization in the society it cannot emerge as an efficient state. Such a perception of a state can only be achieved if the state ensures high participation and is more transparent and accountable in its actions.

An analysis of state on these parameters can be extremely helpful in understanding the nature of state. A state based on these principles will be seen as more representative and therefore more legitimate. Such a state will also be more successful in combating poverty and unemployment. Besides, a legitimate state's laws are more obeyed with the will to followThis reduces the crime tendencies in the state.

However, in the absence of these the state looses its authority and seen as an illegitimate entity. This further hampers implementation of various state plans as well as welfare measures.Above all the crime rates go high as people do not see adequate legal channels to address their grievances. In such conditions they choose illegal ways. In other words, the lack of democratic governance leads to the crisis of governability.

II

UNDERSTANDING STATE IN PRACTICE: THE GOVERNANCE APPROACH

Plato's idea of the philosopher king and   Aristotle's classification of the governments are interpreted as attempts to define and achieve "good governance" for their countrymen. However , the origin of governance as a concept can be traced back to the "sixteenth century and more specifically to the eighteenth century" (Pagden 1998: 10). The concept was also reflected in the writings of German philosopher Immanuel Kant. His concept of 'perpetual peace' was an attempt to discover certain global governance principles.

However, in all these thoughts the meaning of governance was limited to an ideal rather than socio-political or economic phenomenon. The notion of *governance* has reemerged as a significant concept in the late 1990s after the publication of a World Bank report (1997).

The World Bank report, while analyzing causes of failures of its development programs in the African continent, blamed 'bad governance' in the region. The Bank asserted that "bad governance" inhibited economic development, as the conditions required for economic reforms did not exist in the region.   To tackle these problems and to ensure viable economic development, the Bank endorsed the idea of "good governance"Although the World Bank idea was severely criticized on number of grounds but henceforth the concept of governance has emerged as a guiding principle of public-policy.

Meaning of governance depends on the context in which it is being used. As a result it has various meanings. Governance is interpreted dfferently in different disciplines. The existing survey of governance literatures show that broadly it has been defined in four ways (see Figure 1.3). Nevertheless, there is some overlap in these definitions. Rhodes tries to combine all variations over the meaning of governance, proclaiming that his definition "incorporates significant elements of the other uses of governance:

1) Interdependence between organizations. Governance is broader than the government, covering non-state actors. Changing the boundaries of the state meant the boundaries between public, private and voluntary sectors became shifting and opaque.

2) Continuing interactions between network members, caused by the need to exchange resources and negotiate shared purposes.

3) Game like interactions, rooted in trust and regulated by rules of the game negotiated and agreed by network participants.

4) A significant degree of autonomy from the state. The networks are not accountable to the state; they are self-or ganizing. Although the state does not occupy a sovereign position, it can indirectly and imperfectly steer networks"(Rhodes 1997: 28).

The word governance derives from the Latin word "cybern", the same root as in cybernetics: the science of control. In this sense the purpose of state is to coordinate among various players and to establish some sort of equilibrium among them. Governance is recognized as a mechanism for steering societies or economies. Many times emphasis is on the objectives of steering. Although government remains key to the "steering" but it is argued that in governing any society it should do so "from a distance" i.e. taking along other actors as well (Rhodes 2002: 151).

PROCESS

	Public Administration	International Relations	
STEERING	International development agencies	Comparative Politics	**Rules**

RESULTS

Figure 1.3
Different uses of governance concept (Hyden et al. 2007: 13)

Jon Pierre and B. Guy Peters in their study*Governance, Politics and the State* discuss how the available literature on governance focuses on different aspects of it. For them, the studies so far have been focusing on governance in terms of structures i.e. study of various institutions and governance as a process which includes how various structures interact with each other . However what remains neglected is "governance as an analytical framework". Such a meaning of governance demands redefining the whole concept of politics. "It makes us focus attention on things that happen and the ways in which they happen. By so doing it moves the study of politics away from formal concerns." (Pierre and Peters 1999: 24)

Similarly, Goran Hyden and others have made an attempt to explain the practical aspects of governance in an exhaustive analysis of governance in sixteen countries. They argue that so far the concept of governance has not been used but scholars because of the existing complexities associated with it. Defending a governance approach he writes:

> "By moving in this direction (using governance as an analytical tool), we offer the opportunity for new insights into key relationship between politics and development. We do not merely look at issues of interest to specific group or clients.   We do not as studies of democratization do, merely look at issues of how elections foster democracy and how civil society contributes to civil and political liberties. We take a comprehensive view of all the fill dimensions of political process, allowing for a more open investigation of which explanatory variables count where and when." (Hyden *et al* 2007: 3)

Governance as an approach has emerged as a result of various shortcomings of the structuralist and institutionalist social sciences approaches. They focused on the formal and legal aspects of various political institutions whole informal activities and actors were not taken up as important factors. This inadequacy led to the emergence of governance approach, which includes the non-state and private actors along with the formal institutional structure in any society , polity or economy . Furthermore, the governance approach makes the study more dynamic and result oriented rather than just dwelling upon the number of participants. In other words, the "governance is a beginning and not an end in itself" (Pierre and Peters: 2001).

Besides, governance provides a minimum understanding of state-society relations. It emphasizes on four factors: authority , reciprocity, trust and accountability (Kjaer 2006: 164). Governance-approach helps in evaluating the legitimacy of a regime. Kjaer argues that- "The more regime management is characterized by authority, reciprocity, trust and accountability the more it generates legitimacy for the political system, and the more people will participate in the public realm with enthusiasm.

This study attempts to develop a model of governance approach which can explain the nature of transition states better. It combines three significant aspects of governance: its origin, evolution and results. These aspects can be studied at three levels: at the national level, regional level and at the local level. The units of analysis can be different country wise.

Here one question can be raised about the relevance of the UNDP approach to democratic governance.[10] Why the study does not take the UNDP democratic governance completely and it only focuses on certain key variables? The UNDP list of democratic variable incorporates at least fifty variables to measure democratic governance and human development.[11] However, there is a clear overlapping in these variables. Similarly the UNDP distinguishes between democracy and democratic governance. However its definition of democracy is ambiguous as it incorporates various issues which are part of its democratic governance definition as well, such as the participation related variables.

This study on the other hand argues that instead of focusing on democracy building separately, emphasis on democratic governance is a more useful tool and policy perspective. The concept of democratic governance, which is incorporated here in governance approach, on the one hand prevents falling of the concept of democracy in the hands of minimalists. At the same time it

---

[10] UNDP approach defines governance as, "the system of values, policies and institutions by which a society manages its economic, political and social affairs through interactions within and among the state, civil societ y and priv ate sector. It is the wa y a society organizes itself to make and implement decisions—achieving mutual understanding, agreement and action. It comprises the mechanisms and processes for citizens and groups to articulate their interests mediate their differences and exercise their legal rights and obligations. It is the rules, institutions and practices that set limits and provide incentives for individuals, organizations and firms. Governance, including its social, political and economic dimensions, operates at every level of human enterprise, be it the household, village, municipality, nation, r egion or globe. — *UNDP Str ategy Note on Go vernance for Human development, 2000. Available at http://www.undp.org/oslocentre/flagship/ democratic_governance_assessments.html. Accessed on 20 January 2010.*

[11] For UNDP list of democratic governance indicators see Democratic Governance Reader: A Reference for UNDP practitioners. Available on www.undp.org/governance/

also addresses the issue of state capacity as well. In other words, the concept of democratic governance is more inclusive and holistic in nature as compared to the popular notion of democracy .[12]

Procedural aspects try to look into the level of participation and transparency in the process of decision-making over the form and functions of various institutions. While studying institutions the governance approach discusses various facets of institutional functioning. The major institutions which connect the state and society are: political parties, interest groups and civil society.

Thirdly, the governance approach takes into account the people' s perspective about various institutions and their functioning. Here the performance is measured in terms of level of satisfaction and trust in various institutions. Besides, the overall impact of governance practices can be measured with the help of the levels of freedoms and the human development.

In other words the governance approach presents a comprehensive picture of various processes and institutions which are working at various levels in a country undergoing transition. With the help of such analysis the policy makers can identify the problem areas and the future reforms can be initiated accordingly. Hyden argues that "governance can enrich the study of political and economic reform beyond the snapshot presentations that cross-sectional studies of democratization in any other aspect of national development provide" (Hyden 2007: IX).

For the purpose of this study a more comprehensive definition of governance has been selected given by Goran Hyden   *et al*. They define governance as the "formation and stewardship of the formal and informal rules that regulate the public realm, the arena in which state as well as economic and societal actors interact to make decisions." (Hyden et al 2007: 16).

---

[12] For more on the UNDP concept of democratic governance, democracy and human development, see Human Development Report (2002), *Deepening Democracy in a Fragmented World,* (Oxford University Press: New York). Available online, http://hdr.undp.org/en/media/HDR_2002_EN_Complete.pdf

Research Model

In the governance model nature of state is a dependent variable. Capacity and efficiency of a state depends upon the implementation of democratic governance. For the purpose of this study only three major variable of democratic governance are chosen- participation, accountability and transparency. The governance studies focus only on the implementation of these principles once the state structure or the basic framework of governance principles is in place. The post-Soviet countries have not received much attention so far as the governance analysis is concerned. Only the international organizations analysis has been looking into these issues. It has not been given much importance in the literature of comparative politics or economic analysis. Existing complexities as well as certain ambiguities in the governance methods have made it less useful for comparative political scientists. Similarly the literature on economic transition focuses only on the issue of corruption. Accountability and participation issues are not paid adequate attention.

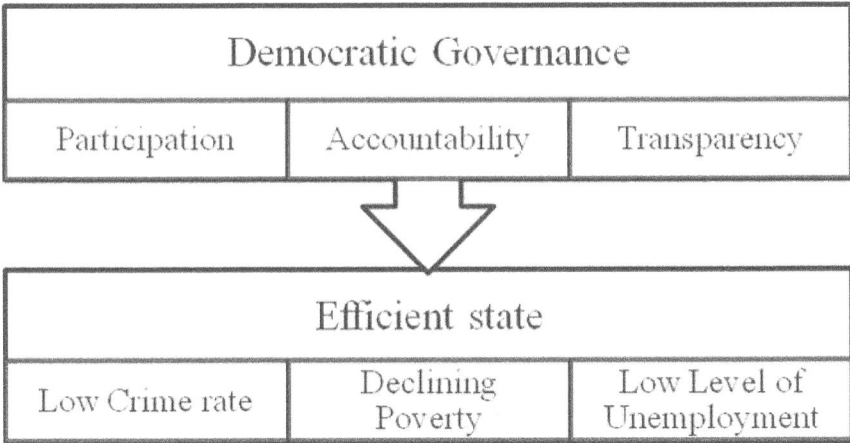

Democratic Governance		
Participation	Accountability	Transparency

Efficient state		
Low Crime rate	Declining Poverty	Low Level of Unemployment

Figure 1.4

The chart above shows various issues of democratic governance which have been lacking in the Russian case. An inefficient state is an outcome of absence of such principles. The table below (see table 1.2) on the other hand shows the list of indicators which have been used in this study to measure the independent and dependent variables.

	Variables	Indicators
Independent variable **Democratic Governance**		
1.	Participation	Constitution making Elections fairness
2.	Transparency	Right to information (Indicator: Whether the information is accessible and constitutionally recognized), Number of decrees
3.	Accountability	Administrative procedures (Selection procedures and availability of independent and autonomous bodies)
Dependent variable **State efficiency**		
4.	Rule of law	Crime rate
5.	Human Development	Poverty and unemployment

Table 1.2

Conclusion

Keeping the Russian case within this framework the study attempts to answer following questions:

    a.   The emerging challenge to the legitimacy and authority of the Russian state;

    b.   Implications of such challenges on the political and economic stability of the Russian state; and

    c.   Reasons behind state failure in effectively controlling these challenges.

In addition to this it will also be an attempt to examine the usefulness of the concept of democratic governance for the study of regime, government and above all the state.

Chapter Two

Russia : A State of Ironies

This book deals with the problems of state-building in the post-Soviet Russia, a task continue to remain daunting even after twenty years of its emergence as an independent state. The Soviet state collapsed due to its failure in providing certain basic minimum to its citizens despite its great promises of economic equality and justice. These basic needs were not simply economic needs, as envisaged in the Marxist philosophy of 'economic determinism.' Rather they were cultural and political in nature as well.

The post-Soviet Russian state emerged with the promise of fulfilling these needs. It promised to build a new state which will ensure economic efficiency, political freedoms and cultural pluralism. A well build, aggressive and former Communist Party leader –Boris Yeltsin was the vanguard of such promises. It was with these hopes that there was extensive support for Yeltsin's revolutionary ideas of change, at least within Russia. Consequently , Yeltsin became a prominent figure in the Soviet policy.

As a result of problems at the political front as well as the weakening economy the Soviet Union collapsed. Russia emerged as a separate state and Boris Yeltsin, who was elected as the President of Russia during the Soviet Union continued to head the post-Soviet Russian state as well. The real test of Yeltsin began now onwards. Whether the new Russia will be able to fulfill the promises which Yeltsin had been making for the last five years? How far Russia will be able to maintain the legacy of Soviet Union as a super power of which it was recognized as a successor? These were some of the questions which the analysts have been trying to answer since emergence of Russia as a separate state after 1991.

However, gradually the optimism started fading away . The Soviet era promises started collapsing one by one. The post-Soviet Russia, instead of making the life of citizens better off failed to provide those basic goods which were available in the Soviet era. Economy collapsed very badly. Agricultural production, industrial output started declining very rapidly. Inflation reached at the all time high level. Many organized crime gangs emerged across the Russian state. Politically the communist dominated Parliament and Yeltsin's presidency were involved in fighting against each other and blaming other for these failures. In short, post-Soviet Russia was in a complete chaos.

The Yeltsin era was full of the challenges described above. In 2000 Yeltsin decided to take retirement. He appointed a former Russian Intelligence official Vladimir Putin as his successor Putin has gained lot of popularity due to his tough handling of Chechen crisis. It was Putin who successfully suppressed the rebellion going on in the Chechen province of Southern Russia which Yeltsin was unable to manage for the first eight years of his presidential rule. Putin was regarded a strong figure unlikeYeltsin who failed to provide a strong take-off to Russia after the Soviet collapse.

The euphoria of Putinism achieved relative success. During Putin's two consecutive presidential terms (2000-2004 and 2004-2008) Russia stabilized on the economic front thanks to increasing global prices of crude oil. Politically Putin managed the parliament in a very clever manner with brining all the main leaders of Russia under one umbrella party , called Unite Russia. In International Politics Russia reasserted its status of a super power which was denied during theYeltsin era. However, almost after a decade of Putinism it is becoming clear that the optimism was of a very short life.

Despite promises of brining Russia' s glory back and establishing 'dictatorship of law', the challenges of the Russian state are not reducing. Crime is still on rise in the country . Racial extremism is emer ging in new forms. Unemployment is still a big challenge. Industries are declining in the absence of latest technology and proper government support.   Above all corruption is a big challenge in Russia. What has made implementation of laws difficult is a growing nexus between politicians, police officials and crime gangs.

This study tries to look into some of these challenges in the post-Soviet Russia. Here an attempt is being made to analyse the factors which have greatly hampered the evolution of an efficient state in the post-Soviet Russia. However what makes Russia a peculiar case is a mismatch between its strengths and weaknesses. Unlike the examples of colonial countries where most of the countries were exploited by the colonial powers Russia has not seen any such past. Its natural resource base is still protected. In fact it has largest oil and gas reserves in the world. Besides, Russia has also got a huge uranium base which is helpful in maintaining its nuclear status in the world. Apart from these natural advantages Russia has developed its institutional and infrastructure base during the tsarist and Soviet Russia. This is an advantage she enjoys over other countries undergoing transition.

This chapter shows how Russia continues to enjoy certain supremacies over other countries which provide it a special position in international affairs. These positives points are also being used at the domestic level by the Russian state. However, lack of a more appropriate and democratic link between the Russian state and society these advantages remained unexplored.

I

RUSSIA : A STRONG STATE

There have been contradictory claims about the Russian state. Some asserted that it was declining after 1991. The major reason behind these assertions was the declining economic conditions in Russia. However in 1999 there was a sudden jump in the international prices of oil. Russia amongst the largest producer of oil and having the largest gas reserves in the world was a big beneficiary. This helped in the revival of Russian economy Since then the oil prices have continued to grow. Consequently the Russian economy has also been growing.

In addition to the economic causes, political analysts believed that the confrontation between the president and the parliament, which was a regular phenomenon during the Yeltsin's regime, would continue. However, learning lessons from Yeltsin's failures, President Putin managed to have a cooperative and friendly parliament. Putin also ensured a state where authority and not anarchy prevails. His strong steps against many tycoons who were quite influential during the previous regime sent a strong message to the Russian elite. In the past they used to manipulate the state machinery as per their interests. Putin's actions reduced these tendencies but could not control it completely.

Putin's attempts to revive the state power in Russia sent a positive message across the world. The country which was decelerating now started rising on the world scenario again. The terminology of 'weak-state' is not used for Russian state any more. Though there are challenges ahead but there are certain advantages which makes Russia a strong state. These factors are as follows:

a.   The Russian Military

According to the Weberian definition a state enjoys unrestrained authority to make law and use coercive force in a defined territory . Police and military forces are two such instruments of coercive force.   A state with a strong military has the strength to impose its will on its citizens. Russian military is amongst the world's top military forces. Though like other institutions the Russian military also faced a phase of decline during the early years of post-Soviet era, especially during the first Chechen war in 1995, but it has also seen revival in the last decade.

Under President Putin, the Russian leadership emphasized the role of a strong military in establishing a strong state. They also felt that strengthening the military lead to an effective foreign policy and convey the image of an active global power capable of asserting it national interests. In 2002 Dmitry Rogozin, the chairman of the foreign affairs committee, a member of a pro-Putin faction in the Duma, stated that Russia had only two reliable allies—the Russian army and the Russian navy. Many others in the Duma have called for increase in Russian military spending as the only way to guarantee respect for Russia in international affairs and a strong state at the domestic level.

By 2007 the Russian defense budget had almost quadrupled to $31 billion over the previous six years. In 2005 Russian defense spending rose 22 percent, 27 percent in 2006 and analysts estimate that in 2007 it could increase by an additional 30 percent. In 2007 the Russian Government approved a re-armament program through the year 2015 with a $240 billion budget. Apart from these improvements in the spending on military a major moral boost upwas its victory in the Chechnya war in 1999. The Russian army successfully crushed the terrorist groups which were functioning in the Chechnya region. Since then it has been actively involved in ensuring stability in the region. Although the problems of separatist movement continue in Chechnya but this has sent a strong message to other Russian regions that might have started demanding more freedom or autonomy in the absence of a strong response to the Chechen problem.

b.   A Strong Natural Resource Base

Russia's oil and gas sector

The factor which has been the source of strength to the Russian state is its oil and gas reserves and industry In last few years Russian economy has expanded faster than many developed economies of the world thanks to the increase in Russian oil production and relatively high world oil prices.

According to the *Oil and Gas Journal's 2008 survey,* Russia has proven oil reserves of 60 billion barrels, most of which are located in Western Siberia, between the Ural Mountains and the Central Siberian Plateau.

With production of 9.8 million bbl/d and consumption of just 2.8 million bbl/d, Russia exported around 7 million bbl/d. according to official Russian statestics, roughly 4.4 million bbl/d of this total is crude oil. Over 70 percent of Russian crude oil production is exported while the remaining 30 percent is refined locally.

Most of Russia's product exports consist of fuel oil, which are exported mainly to European countries and, on a small scale to the United States. Russian oil exports to the U.S. have almost doubled since 2004, rising to over 400,000 bbl/d of crude oil and products in 2007.

Updated monthly and annual data are available from EIA 's Petroleum Navigator. Increases in product exports can be attributed to political pressure to maintain refinery operations and higher international oil pricesA draft plan for the refining sector 's development for 2005-2008 foresees continued increases in the production of high quality light oil products, catalysts and raw material for the petrochemical industry.

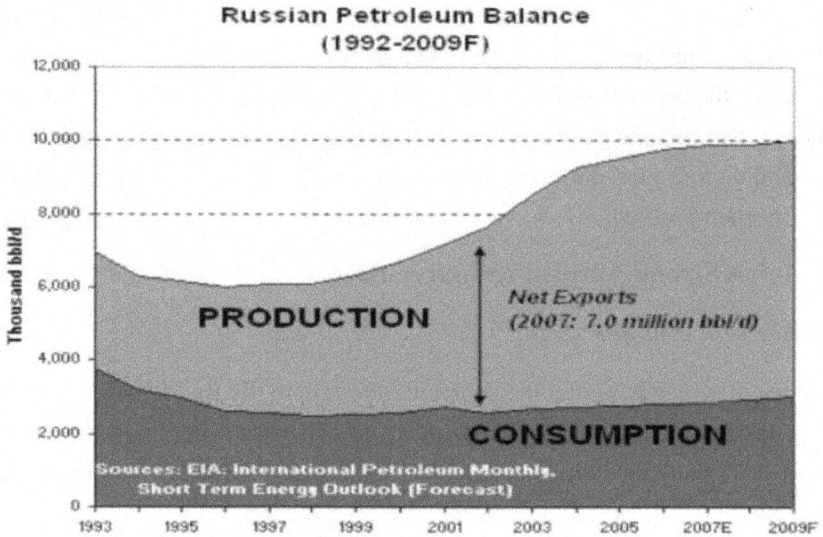

Figure 2.1
Russia's Oil Pr oduction
Source: Energy Information Administration available at www .eia.doe.gov.com

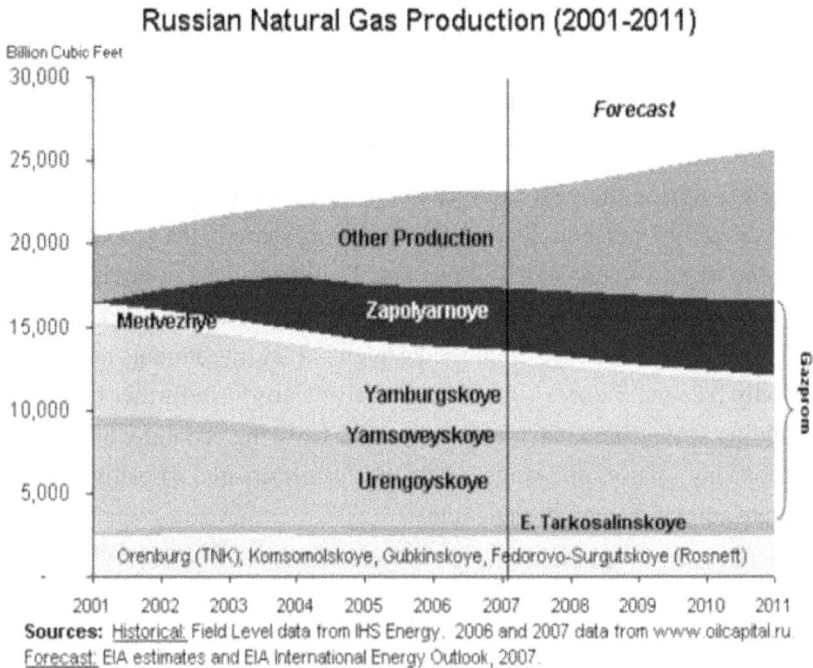

Figure 2.2
Russia's Gas Pr oduction
Source: Energy Information Administration available at www .eia.doe.gov.com

According to the *Oil and Gas Journal's* 2008 survey, Russia holds the world's largest natural gas reserves, with 1,680 trillion cubic feet (Ϯf), which is nearly twice the reserves in the next lar gest country, Iran. In 2006 Russia was the world's largest natural gas producer (23.2 Tcf), as well as the world's largest exporter (6.6 Tcf). According to official Russian statistics, production during 2007 totaled around 23.1   Tcf, of which 85 percent (19.4   Tcf) was produced by Gazprom. Russian government forecasts expect gas production to total 31.1 Tcf by 2030.

As a result of these developments in the last one decade, the Russian state has negated all the predictions of its collapse or meltdown. Rather it has reemerged as a strong economic and political player in the global politics. It has successfully reasserted its role as a great power. Though its strengths are limited yet it remains a key actor in international politics.

Russia has great potential for faster economic development thanks to its natural resource base. The Russian economy which was in the crisis till 1998 has shown remarkable revival.   The industrial production was declining; agriculture production went below the Soviet levels. However   , by 2000 it started achieving excellent growth rate. Figure 5.1 shows various economic indicators during the year 2000 to 2005. The average growth rate was approximately 7 percent. During this period its share in the global economy has gone from 2.7 percent to 3.2 percent. The Russian economy is the seventh biggest economy of the world. Its foreign exchange reserves are the second largest in the world. Since 2000 the Foreign Direct Investments have gone up radically (see the Figure).   All these positive signs have further helped in rebuilding strong state machinery in Russia. Growing economy has resulted in increasing salaries and wages. This has further created a positive image of the state among the common people.

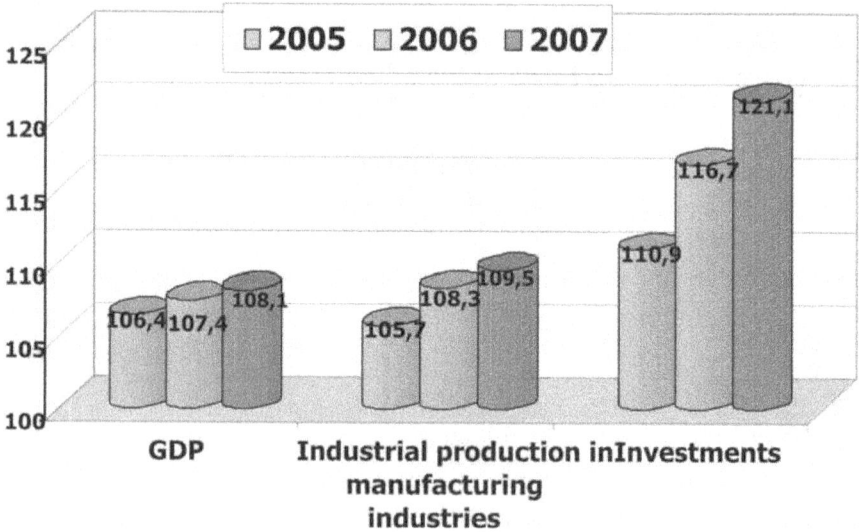

Figure 2.3
Russia: Economic Growth
Source: Ministry of Russian Federation for Economic Development and T   rade

II

RUSSIA : A WEAK STATE

What has restrained Russia's emergence as a super power is the problems at home. It continues to suffer from the crisis of governance which has resulted in a weak state at the domestic front. Despite various economic successes these benefits have not reached a major section of the Russian society . The next section discusses these problems in more detail.

The authority of Russian state has been facing serious resistance from various regions. There are a large numbers of cases of violation of the federal constitution by the regional governments. This has been identified as even the 'federal collapse' of the Russian federation. [1] Though Moscow claims that it has brought the situation in the North Caucasus under control, the terrorist attacks are on rise despite all its military efforts. Till 2007, the Russian army has lost at least 10,000 soldiers and policemen, and 80,000 civilians in its war on terrorism in Chechnya.[2] Apart from the terrorist attacks the crime rate has also gone up exponentially in the previous decade. There has been opposition for the government's economic policies and political set up. All these are the indicators of the problem of weakness of the Russian state in performing its primary task i.e. governing its territory.

After the collapse of the Soviet state, new Russia emerged as the world's most crime affected country. The nature of crime has been diverse in nature. All types of crime, ranging from small thefts to political violence have gone up in the last one and half decade of transition of Russia. Number of crime

---

[1] Graeme P. Herd (1999), "Russia: Systemic Transformation or Federal Collapse?", *Journal of Peace Research* (36:3), 259-269. Herd discusses the emerging federal system in Russia. He argued that with the present trends Russia is moving towards either a weak federation of a conf ederation. However, Mikhail Alexeev counters this argument and defends the policies followed by the president Putin to save the Russian federation. Mikhail Alexeev (2001), "Decentralization versus State Collapse: Explaining Russia's Endurance, *Journal of Peace Research,* 38:1, 101-106.

[2] For a more detailed analysis on Russia's war against Chechnya and terrorism in North Caucasus see the Russian Analytical Digest, *The North Caucasus,* No. 22, 5 June 2007 . Also see No. 5, 29August 2006, *Beslan and After*

cases which were approximately 2000 in the year 1992 has gone up to 3500 in 2005 (See the table below).

The biggest challenge before the Russian government is how to ensure that the laws in the federal units are in accordance with the federal constitution. In a study of the relations between the centre and the units it is shown that the Russian Ministry of Justice created a registry of over 100,000 regional "normative acts" – which includes laws and other government decisions— and in 2001 reviewed over 52,000. Over 5,000 unconstitutional acts of regions were invalidated between mid-2000 and the end of 2001. [3] It was reported that in Bashkortostan, 72 percent of the existing laws and decrees violated federal law. Similarly in Tatarstan there was strong resistance from the republic legislature and executive to ef forts to force it to conform to federal law . In Yakutia, officials had been able to ignore the 1995 Law on Local Self-Management, as of 2002 the region did not have elected local government bodies. The preferred solution of many regional leaders was for the federal centre to revise its legislation to conform with *their* laws (Slider 2003: 127).

	1992	1995	2000	2001	2002	2003	2004	2005
Number of criminal cases	1149	1596	1741	1644	1258	1237	1223	1297
By the age 14-15	59.3	69.2	49.3	51.9	40.1	43.2	46	44.6
16-17	129	139	129	121	100	102	106	105
18-24	252	363	465	441	348	359	348	365
25-29	186	231	289	273	199	200	202	224
30-49	523	792	676	625	463	436	425	454
50 and over	-	-	133	132	108	96.1	96.3	106

Table 2.1 Crime in Russia
Source: Ministry of Interior

[3] Available at www.strana.ru, Visited on February 30, 2002.

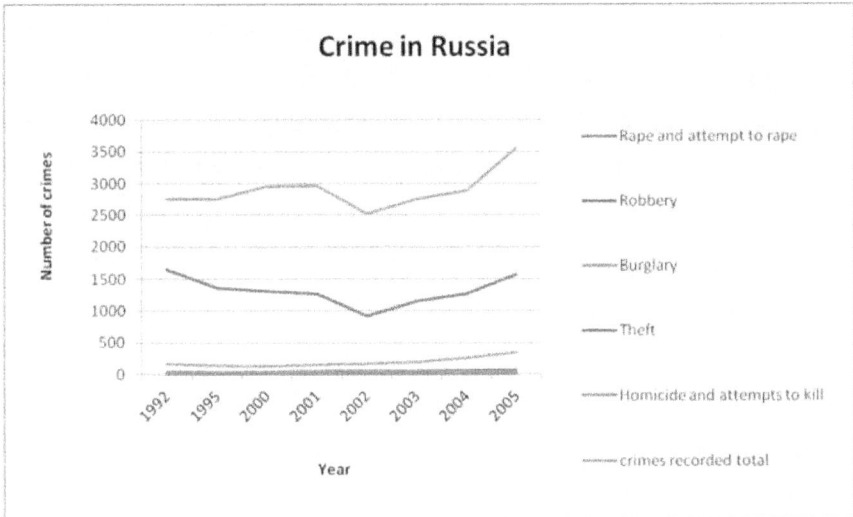

Crime in Russia

Number of crimes

4000
3500
3000
2500
2000
1500
1000
500
0

1992 1995 2000 2001 2002 2003 2004 2005

Year

Rape and attempt to rape

Robbery

Burglary

Theft

Homicide and attempts to kill

crimes recorded total

Figure 2.4
Source: Ministry of Interior

In addition to this, the growing crime rate is another serious challengeA major reason behind increasing crime rate is the decline of law enforcing agencies and increasing problems of unemployment and poverty. The Police and other law enforcing agencies have become so corrupt that after becoming the current president Dmitri Medvedev declared reforms in the police as its primary agenda. In an opinion poll on corruption in Russia, 59 percent of the respondents said that the militia, police and customs are the most corrupt agencies in the new Russia. [4] Decline of these agencies have led to higher crime rates. This phenomenon was more prevalent in the metro cities especially in the St. Petersburg [5] which was recognized once as the crime capital of Russia. Russian criminal groups were a serious threat not only to the Russian government but also to the world peace and stability . The US department of Justice in its report in 2001 recognized the organized Russian crime as the

---

[4] Opinion poll conducted by the "Public Opinion Foundation" (FOM) conducted in December 2005, and published by the Russian Analytical Digest No 11, December 5, 2006.

[5] In a wonderful travelogue, Andrew Meier discusses nature of Russian crime. Andrew has discussed some of his personal experiences during his long stay in Russia (*The Black Earth* (2004).

emerging transnational threat which may have serious repercussions for the US, Eastern and Western Europe and Israel. It states:

Russian organized crime has come to plague many areas of the globe since the demise of the Soviet Union just more than a decade ago. The transnational character of Russian organized crime, when coupled with its high degree of sophistication and ruthlessness, has attracted the world' s attention and concern to what has become known as a global Russian Mafia[6]

What is more challenging is increasing criminal tendencies amongst the Russian youth. The highest crime rate has been registered amongst the age group of 30-49. In this age the youth is expected to perform many family responsibilities. But due to increasing prices of essential goods and insecure employment it has become dif ficult in present day Russia. As a result the youths are forced to turn to crimes. Declining education standards and lack of good employment opportunities in the far away areas of Russia has also resulted in the increasing crime rates among the students (see the table 2.1).

The nature of crime in Russia is also extremely serious (See the chart below). Contract killings are quite common phenomenon in the Russian cities. Apart from their crime activities the crime groups are also involve in the economic activities.[7] Capital markets are heavily dominated by organized crime. The organized crime in diversified in all regions of the country Criminals are also taking part in the political activities. (Shelley 2003: 103-122)

In this respect, since the urban areas are more developed with better employment opportunities, the crime is more prominent in the rural areas. Though organized crime is a more prominent phenomenon in big cities but the overall crime rate is higher in the rural areas than in the urban areas. Further, overall crime rates are higher in the Eastern part of Russia than in the western or northern part. Southern Russia is more vulnerable to organized

---

[6] James O. Finckenauer and Yuri A. Voronin (2001), "The Threat of the R ussian Organized Crime", (US Department of Justice), W ashington.

[7] Shelley, Louise I. (2003), "The Challenge of Crime and Corruption" in Stephen K. W egren, ed., *Russia's Policy Challenges: Security, Stability and Development,*(Armonk: M.E. Sharpe): 103-122.

and violent crime or terrorist activities. These areas have also been suffering from the problem of economic underdevelopment and administrative negligence. As a result dissatisfaction among the youth has led to higher crime rates.

Shelley argues that problems of crime and corruption are not simply failures of law enforcement agencies in Russia. Rather it is linked to the inability of domestic as well as international agencies' to understand the 'systemic approaches to preventing problems'. In stead of involving all the sections of society in the reform process the international agencies and Yeltsin preferred to work with a small group of oligarchs who dominated banking, the media and Russia's natural resources. They in turn by passed parliament and ignored issues of democratic governance.

On the economic front also the Russian state has failed to protect the economic well being of its citizens. After initial decline in the revenues the Russian economy recovered in 2000 thanks to increasing petroleum rates.As the international petroleum prices grew the Russian GDP also increased at the similar pace. However, with the decline in the petroleum prices the Russian economy has also started loosing its growth. In the first quarter of year during 2001-2006, its GDP has started declining.

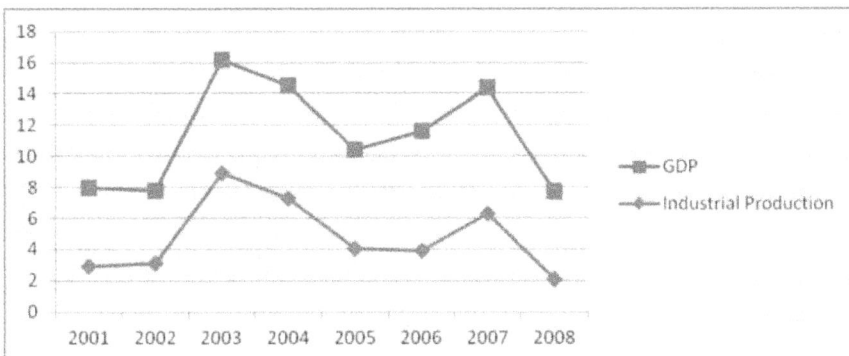

Figure 2.5: GDP and Industrial Production
Source: Russian Federal Ser vice of S tate Statistics (www.gks.ru)

During the 1990s the Russian economy had undergone radical changes. Every year the economy shrank and price of necessary goods approached hyperinflationary levels. By the time of the ruble crisis of 1998 Russian GDP had fallen by 42 percent and poverty had risen from 2 percent of the population to over 40 percent. This proved the fragility of the Russian economy . The government was unable to collect tax revenue to cover its expenditures. As a result the budget deficit rose to about 8 percent. The shortfall in tax revenues resulted in part from the enormous subsidies still paid to loss-making enterprises; the government had not been able adequately to cut its expenses, even though it collected (although arbitrarily and incompetently) some one-third of GDP in tax revenues, similar to the US level.[8]

Economic reforms, instead of strengthening democracy have weakened it. As per the neo-liberal notion it was expected that implementation of liberal economic programs will lead to a country wide economic development. It was also expected that this will also be helpful in the development of various regions of Russia.

On the contrary , the regions have been less than willing to send their revenues to the central government. Economic policies to decentralize the Russian economy have made corruption more sophisticated at the regional level, with more money to divert from federal programs. This problem is epitomized in the Russian far-east, which receives one of the largest shares as an intermediary for the export of capital. Officials and organized crime groups on the regional level have established direct links abroad and developed more complicated mechanisms to enrich themselves and to cover their illicit and semi-illicit activities (Shelley 2005: 102)

Unlike, economic decentralization centralization of political power has further led to decline of federal tax structure. The centralization of executive and legislative powers in Moscow generated dissatisfaction among the regions in Russia. Introduction of a new system would have threatened the position of elites who were enjoying privileges during the Soviet period. These elites

---

[8] "Bulk of Russians avoid paying taxes", Radio Free Europe/ Radio Liberty Newsline, 3(138) (July 19, 1999).

were against such reforms or were trying to sabotage the existing system. The real challenge before the new leadership was to create a social base for these reforms. But no such attempts were made to generate popular support in favor of reforms. Instead, the new leadership decided to go for bargaining with these regional leaders. The 1992 federal treaty was an outcome of such bargaining. However, this provided an opportunity to the old Soviet elite to misuse the whole process of reform. This section, while misusing their political position, is now deeply involved in corruption and malpractices.

This indicated the failure of Russian state in ensuring a better life of its citizens. Despite implementing the neo-liberal economic reforms and bringing a western style liberal constitutional democracy the Russian state has yet not been able to come out of the problems which resulted into the collapse of the Soviet state.

The widely studied issues about the transition of the post-Soviet Russia are; one, implementation of the neo-liberal economic policies, and two building a constitutional liberal democracy. The former has been an area of focus for the economists who have been looking into the challenges of building a market economy.[9] The latter on the other hand focuses on the issue of democracy building.

The studies on democracy building in Russia broadly focus on two issues: first, creation of representative institutions (like the parliament, the political parties, the civil society and so on) and second, the nature of regime. This literature has largely contributed to the explanations of the nature of emerging political institutions, role of the leadership and impact of regime on the institutions and political processes. A major focus of the literature on the regime has been on the emergence of autocracy in Russia and how the political institutions are being dominated by the presidency.[10]

---

[9] For example Aslund et al (1996), Negi (1997).

[10] For example studies by V alerie B unce, Michael McF aul, K athryn Stioner-Weiss (2010), Micael McF aul (2001), Stev en M Fish (1999, 2001), V alerie B unce (1998, 1995), Nei l Robinson (2005), Thomas F. Remington (2002), Timothy Colton (2003) etc.

However, these analyses are unable to provide adequate explanations to the question of the nature of state and its relationship with the emerging governance mechanisms. Moreover , many significant issues which have serious implications for democracy building and economic development continue to remain neglected. Issues like crime, regional inequality, growing poverty and unemployment are not adequately discussed. This study attempts to bring some of such issues to the forefront. [11]

In fact there are certain more relevant questions about Russia requiring urgent and serious attention, such as: How the Russian state has failed to evolve as an efficient state? What are the major challenges before the authority of the post-Soviet Russian state? What are the major reasons behind the present crisis of governability? Why the existing literature has failed to touch upon the issue of declining authority of the Russian state?

The studies on the nature of Russian state which are recent in origin have made certain attempts to look into some of these crucial issues. However, these studies are narrow in their focus as they largely discuss the issues of politics and the state only . The most significant question of nature of any state i.e. who governs and how , yet remains untouched. This study ar gues that despite various claims of rebuilding the governance structures, the basic nature of the Russian state continues to remain as it was during the Soviet era.

---

[11] There are arguments against any correlation between the governance capacity and democracy. It has been argued that administr ative capacity can be achieved and main-tained even without democracy building. In fact it is this assertion which becomes the basis of the argument which favors 'good governance' (defined in terms of higher administrative capacity to deli ver) over a democr atic polity. However in a study b y Black and Hadenuis (2002) it has been argued that in the initial stages of democracy building the level of democracy is negatively affected from declining administrative capacity. But after a period of time it leads to faster growth in the level of administrative capacity. This study is based on the argument that democracy in the form of widely accepted principles of 'democratic governance' is essential in or der to achieve higher administr ative capacity. Howev er, democracy with its popular form i.e. the minimalist democracy may not result into adminis-trative capacity. India is a prime example of this category . See Atul Kohli (1990), *Democracy and Discontent: India's Growing Crisis of Governability* (Cambridge University Press: New York).

[12] For example Kathryn Stoner-Weiss (2006), *Resisting the State: Reform and Retrench-ment in Post-Soviet Russia* , (Cambridge: Cambridge University Press).

Conclusion

The Russian state is still being governed by a small section of the elite. Entry for the new actors in this system is still restricted. Though in theory a representative democracy based on the principles of multi-party democracy is in place, in reality the Russian state is unaccountable and non transparent in its practices. With the introduction of a representative democracy the whole affair is managed in a very crafty manner.[13]

The policies devised in the name of building a strong and efficient state in Russia end up negatively impacting the state ef ficiency. The government policies favor only a smaller section of the population confined to some selected regions. This is reflected in the growing problem of regional inequality across the country. Such inequalities have led to growing dissatisfaction amongst the Russian youth. The present political and administrative set up has failed to emerge as an ef fective platform for expression of people' s will. This has further resulted into growing cases of crime and violence in various regions of Russia. After Iraq and Pakistan, Russia has lost largest number of people in various criminal and terrorist incidents in the last one decade.

---

[13] For this reason many scholars char acterized Russia as a case of 'managed democr acy.'

Chapter Three

Russia's Unfair Participatory Procedures: Constitution Making and Elections

In the democratization literature elections are the focal point of analysis for measuring participation. Certainly elections are crucial. However, apart from the elections what determines the nature of participation in a state is the level of inclusion of society in the process of 'goal setting.' (Peters 2004: 29) All the countries which came into existence after the collapse of the Soviet Union including Russia started adopting new constitutions. However, what has hampered the process of state building is, what Peter Burnell (2006) calls 'autocratic opening.' This is done with ignoring the principles of good governance at the initial level of formation of the new state structure. With the adoption of principles of democratic governance (transparency, accountability and participation) various social groups could have been included into the political process establishing a better relationship between the state and society.

However, instead of connecting state with the society in Russia this process strengthened nexus between the Soviet era elite and the emerging elite in the name of democracy. Another significant step towards building a more participatory governance system and state are the elections. In the post-Soviet Russia elections are not means of change but to strengthen the existing ruling elite or political regime. Failure of both these significant participatory mechanisms has generated a feeling of alienation in many sections of society resulting into the 'legitimacy crises' for the Russian state.

I

UNDEMOCRATIC BEGINNING: CONSTITUTION MAKING IN POST-SOVIET RUSSIA

In the initial years of transition in Russia the priority was given to economic reforms and not to the political restructuring. [1] In the new Russia no serious actions were taken by the elite to foster deliberations and to build any consensus amongst various political sections. In fact, the first two years of transition can be categorized as the phase of strengthening of the presidency under Boris Yeltsin. The issue of constitution making was not considered as a serious issue. As Vladimir Mau, an advisor to Gaidar (Gaidar was the brain behind economic reforms and adoption of 'shock-therapy approach') at the time recalled:

'At this moment (the end of 1991) - whether consciously or subconsciously- there is a principal decision made, the reforms of the political system are halted. If in 1988-89 political reforms was first priority of Gorbachev and his close associates, nowYeltsin decides to freeze the situation, to preserve the status-quo regarding the or ganization of state-power ' (Mau as quoted in MacFaul 2001: 146).

Even R.I. Khasbulatov, the second highest ranking leader after Yeltsin also declared that the economic reforms were of prime importance compared to political restructuring. [2] Immediately after the coup attempt, the new chairman of the Russian Congress Ruslan Khasbulatov repeatedly identified himself as "Yeltsin's closest ally." [3] In this addressYeltsin outlined his economic plans for a new Russian economy. He made it clear, that he is 'not afraid of

---

[1] It seems that the Russian political leaders were more influenced from the modernization thesis of liberal democr acy (see Sudhir K umar, upcoming publication, *Democratization Theories Revisited: The Post-Soviet Experience*). The modernization theory argues that economic development is a k ey determinant of evolution of democr acy. Higher the economic development is, more the possibilities of democratic survival and sustenance of democracy.

[2] Interview with Ruslan Khasbulatov , "I don' t think ther e is any real danger of a leftist dictatorship", (Published in *Pravada*, Sept. 10), *Current Digest of the Soviet Press (CDSP),* Vol. XLII, No. 38 (1991), p . 35.

[3] See the interview with Khasbulatov in *Sovetskaya Rossiya,* December 4, 1990.

accusations of being undemocratic' because his primary task is to implement economic reforms. [4]

Political reforms were regarded as the secondary goal by the reformists. For them, it served no other purpose except increasing their bargaining capacity. In other words, politics in itself was not a desirable activity for public good. Rather individual bargaining and distribution of benefits, positions and other tactics were approved to take acceptance of various regional elites. During this whole process certain premises of debates and discussions were ignored. The Russian elite felt no need to overcome what Fearon (1998: 49) calls 'the bounded rationality'. The notion of bounded rationality believes that our imaginations and calculating abilities were limited and fallibleYeltsin and his team were under the impression that they are putting a 'final solution' of the problems which people had been facing in the Soviet period. The questions rose by the parliamentarians and the members of the Communist Party were dismissed as being nothing but their anger and frustration against the emerging Yeltsin regime. Yeltsin accused the parliament for being anti-reformist who were against the economic reforms.

In the post-Soviet Russia multi-party elections were recognized as the first steps towards the promotion of democracy . Holding the new elections could have been the most appropriate step to bring new political forces in the parliament. Besides, it would have also given a new beginning to the reform process in the country. Yeltsin, however, decided not to hold elections which were due in December 1991.

Amidst these conditions, an opportunity for broadening the mass base for democracy building emerged. It was the time of elections for the regional legislatures, which were to be held in October 1991 as per the schedule. This could have served as a good opportunity to receive a fresh mandate from various corners of Russia. New people could have been selected from the newly elected legislatures who could be incorporated in the process of constitution making. In many countries, the constituent assembly was chosen by the regional legislatures.A similar method could have been used for Russia

---

[4] Ibid.

as well. Ironically, Yeltsin requested the parliament to delay these elections for a year or so. For him, it was not the right time to hold elections due to the winter and the unstable political condition.[5]

This was the first step towards ignoring or delaying the political reform process, though many of Yeltsin's advisors suggested him to hold elections as many East European countries did. Many believed that the perfect time for a "founding election" was right after the communist collapse. The leaders of Democratic Russia were particularly enthusiastic about holding elections because they believed that elections in winters would produce several positive political results. Democratic Russia polling indicated that their organization, with Yeltsin's endorsement, would win a majority within the Congress of People's Deputies, if elections were held before the economic reforms were implemented.

Yeltsin and his closest advisors rejected the idea of early elections for several reasons. First, the leaders of independent Russia believed that their newly created state did not have the capacity to carry out a national election. In the initial weeks of its existence, the Russian state did not have such elementary resources as funding for printing of ballots or administrative capacity to organize and appoint electoral commissions.

Secondly, Yeltsin argued that the state was in a bad condition and was incapable of carrying out the elections. And third, Yeltsin and his associates did not believe that new elections would produce a reformist parliament or bring Yeltsin's loyalists at the regional level. FinallyYeltsin and his government feared that new elections might fuel Russian federal dissolution, just as elections at the republic level in 1990 had helped to catalyze Soviet federal dissolution. Among these fears, Yeltsin decided to postpone the elections.

In Moscow various political leaders such as: A. Volsky, G. Popov, A. Sobchak, E. Shevardnadze, S. Shatalin, and A. Yakovlev favored Yeltsin's move to implement economic reforms. But they also criticized the president

---

[5] "Appeal to the Russian SFSR Supreme Soviet in Connection with the Adoption of The RSFSR Law 'On Elections f or Administration Chief'": Boris Yeltsin (Published text in *Rossiiskaya Gazeta,* October 18, p. 1), *CDSP,* Vol. XLII, No. 42 (1991), p. 11.

for his undemocratic measures. Many leaders expressed their speculations about the emergence of new-authoritarianism in the new Russia. [6] However, all these speculations remained unheard.

However, the real reason for not holding the elections was Yeltsin's fear of loosing his dominance in the new polity if new actors emerge after the elections. So far the state' s ability is concerned during this period   Yeltsin assured the parliament and people that the new Russian state is capable enough to implement and manage radical economic reforms. [7] Contradictory to his own defence of postponing the regional elections, in his address to the parliament said:

> 'The situation in Russia is difficult but not hopeless. There is no reason for panic. The time has come to adopt the main decision and to begin to act.' [8]

It was a real opportunity to build consensus over the issues of political and economic reforms but Yeltsin really suspected the outcome of the elections. These elections would have helped in the creation of a federation based on shared sovereignty, rather than imposed by some authorities who were elected during the Soviet era. Richard Sakwa argues that elections at this time would have "reinforced Yeltsin's dependency on Democratic Russia and the 'democratic movement' as a whole: and as a corollary   , the deepening of democratic revolution would have entailed an assault against the nomenklatura class, something Yeltsin was loathe to do since he soon came to rely on precisely these managerial and administrative elites (Sakwa 1996: 103). In reality, Yeltsin tactically mar ginalized Democratic Russia and democratic movement as a whole.

---

[6] The Democr atic R ussia leader Y akovlev expressed these speculations during the meet. Other key leaders also expressed similar fears. For details, see, "But Will There Be Re-forms", (Published in *Kuranty*, Dec. 17, pp. 1-4), *CDSP*, Vol XLIII, No. 50 (1991) p. 19.

[7] See note 8.

[8] "Boris Yeltsin: I pledge to my people that a reform cabinet will be formed, and I am counting on understanding and support from the deputies and every resident of the Russian repub-lic." (Published in *Izvestia,* October 28), *CDSP,* Vol. XLIII, No. 43, November 27, 1991, p. 1.

At the sixth session of Congress of People' s Deputies in April 1992, several draft constitutions were tabled. The deputies circulated a draft constitution; the parliament' s draft proposed a parliamentary republic that gave broad powers to the president, counterbalanced with legislature' s and judiciary's powers. Sergei Shakrai, Yeltsin's legal advisor put forward a draft known as the "president's draft". This version subordinated the legislature to the presidential administration. Other draft constitutions, one by Anatoly Sobchak, Mayor of St. Petersburg, and Sergei Alekseyev were also circulated. These drafts promoted the executive powers in comparison to the parliament. After discussion, the parliament rejected the parliamentary and Sobchak' s draft. It accepted only some general principles of the Constitutional Commission's proposals and called for a new draft. The Constitutional Commission then, brought out a fourth version in November 1992. But this draft was also not accepted by the 7 th CPD in December 1992.

Three different versions of constitution making procedures emerged in the debate over the adoption of the new constitution. First, the present Congress should draft the new constitution. Initially the parliament especially various communist groups favoured this option but later they started demanding a dominating role of the parliament in drafting. [9] Two, there should be a new constituent assembly elected through holding new elections. The Democratic Russia was an advocate of this option. Thirdly, there can be a referendum in which people should be given an option to decide that how the new constitution should be made.

Russia's regions were also sidelined from the whole process of constitution making. Though there opinion was accepted on some issues which were not of great significance but they were ignored on the important question. For instance, on the issue of referendum Yeltsin made a direct appeal to the people of Russia. However after completing his speech in the Congress when Yeltsin left the hall he was followed by only 120 deputies. This gave an indication to Yeltsin that the Congress is not in his favour Therefore he decided

---

[9] Ruslan Khasbulatov, "The Congr ess of P eople's deputies and consti tutional r eform", *Rossiskaya Gazea, January 9, pp. 1-2,* in CDPSP, Vol XLV, No.2., 1993, p. 7-9.

to be liberal and accepted Chernomyrdin as a Prime Minister candidate instead of Yegor Gaidar.

The republics were more in favour of fresh elections rather than creation of a constituent assembly or conference. As soon as Yeltsin became sure that he can manage without some of the regional leaders he imposed his own constitution commission and constitution.

What is significant here is that both institutions of power were trying to address the public opinion directly . In other words, they were not ready to negotiate and reach out at a political solution to various problems including the question of basic principles of the constitution. Besides,Yeltsin as well as Khasbulatov were trying to hold their positions on the one hand, and not really keen to be accountable to the other branch of the power. Yeltsin didn't want a stronger parliament because it would have hampered his own power . Khasbulatov wanted a strong parliament as he considered himself as the sole leader of the Congress.

In order to arrive at some compromiseYeltsin appointed a Constitutional Conference. This body consisted of experts from various streams along with leaders from all the political parties and representatives from Russia'regions. However, like other efforts this was also nothing but an attempt to bring all sections in favour of Yeltsin's choice and therefore Yeltsin himself appointed all the members of the Conference. Even all opposition leaders were invited to join the Conference (McFaul 2002: 192). It was also an attempt to bypass the efforts of the parliament for formulating a new constitution. Since president himself appointed all the members of the Conference, it never received serious attention.

However, Yeltsin decided to proceed with his own plan of referendum. While preparing for the referendum not only   Yeltsin but Congress as well declared it as a vote on the role of president. He proposed four questions in the referendum which was held on 25ᵗʰ April 1993:

1. *Do you trust Russian president Yeltsin?*

2. *Do you approve of the socio-economic policy conducted by the Russian president and by the Russian government since 1992?*

3. *Should the new pr esidential election be conducted earlier than scheduled?*

4. *Should the new parliamentary election be conducted earlier than scheduled?*

The results of referendum changed the overall scenario as it gaveYeltsin a clear vote of confidence. [10] This was a clear victory for   Yeltsin, of his economic policies, and a political system in which the President will have a greater role to play.

Yeltsin proposed his own draft, which was clearly in favor of a strong presidential system. The draft envisaged the abolition of the old Congress and the Supreme Soviet, and their subsequent replacement by a bicameral legislature.[11] This draft was also rejected by the parliament. This was severely criticized by Khasbulatov and his followers. He labelled the draft as a 'Tsarist constitution' where President will be a 'Monarch'. The Congress decided to cut-down the powers of the president. In a constitutional amendment proposal, the Congress proposed to reduce many powers of the president. [12]

Yeltsin appointed Chief of the S taff Sergei Filatov as the Head of the constitution Draft Commission. They drew inspiration from earlier versions of constitutions presented before the parliament during 1991-1993. They also took some parts from volumes of work that had been produced by the Constitutional Conference, and from the Rumyantev draft produced in the

---

[10] Election Data were published in Izvestia which shown that out of 64.8 percent voting Yeltsin r eceived around 58 percent   of votes in his f avor. (See *Izvestia*, April 28, p.2), *CDPSP,* Vol. XLV, No. 17, May 26, 1993, p . 1.

[11] "Constitutional Conference: On a Democratic Russian State System and the Draft of a New Constitution: Speech by Boris Y eltsin, President of the R ussian Federation", (Published in *Rossiiskiye vesti*, June 8, 1993), *CDPSP,* Vol. XCLV, No. 23, July 7, 1993.

[12] The Eighth (Extraordinary) Congress of Russian Federation People's Deputies, (The text of constitutional amendments published in *Rossiiskiye Gazeta,* March 13), *CDPSP,* Vol XLV, No. 10 (1993), p.11.

past by the Constitutional Commission of the Russian Congress of People' s Deputies. InAugust, 1993, a combined group of the Constitutional Conference and former members of the parliamentary Constitutional Conference reconvened, and formally served on the drafting committee of the new constitution, although Yeltsin's aides began to dominate the process.

Use of Force and rejection of the existing institutions structure

In order to opposeYeltsin and mobilize support of the deputies and people the Congress decided to stay in their offices in the White House building. The parliament declared Rutskoi, and not Khasbulatov , as the new president of Russia. On the other hand, many supporters of democracy and the parliament were gathered outside the white House in defence of the parliamentary sovereignty. Yeltsin's action of dissolving the Congress and issuing the decree was considered as unconstitutional by majority of Russians. For instance, *Sovetskaya Rossiya* reported on September 23, 1993 that 53 regional Soviets had refused to recognize Yeltsin's decree dissolving the Congress. [13]

More shocking was the role played by the political parties. When the parliamentarians decided to fight for the parliamentary sovereignty   , the strongest opposition party the CPRF decided to stay away from it. Similarly, the Civic Union, another party also decided not to take part in the conflict.

Now Rutskoi ordered the army to take control of major government buildings, started with the house of the Mayor of Moscow   . After initial hesitation, Yeltsin also ordered the army to attack the   White House. After some bombardment, the army took control of the White House and evacuated the building from the parliamentarians. The members of the association share (and it is common knowledge that they share) the view that the appropriate terms of association provide a framework for or are the results of their deliberation. They share, that is, a commitment to coordinating their activities within institutions that make deliberation possible and according to norms that they arrive at through their deliberation. For them, free deliberation among equals is the basis of legitimacy.

---

[13] "Dom Sovetov, Khronika sobytii", *Sovetskaya Rossiya,* September 25, 1993.Macfaul: 196.

During the phase of 1991-93, the parliament was the supreme body and executive organs, including the president and the ministers were accountable to the parliament. However, during the reform process the ministers behaved as the subordinates of the president and ignored the parliamentary legislation.[14] The parliament compromised with its own rules of functioning while discussing or voting on the issue related to the presidential powers. Even there were instances when the chairman of the Supreme Soviet counted the vote of the non-members.[15] Besides, Ruslan Khasbulatov misused his position against his opponents within the parliament. Though the parliament was not always against the choices made by the president and it tried its level best to defend its constitutional position. Apart from the fact that it supported the president on the issue of economic reforms and inclusion of liberal values, individual freedom, and liberty in the new constitution, it also tried to incorporate Yeltsin's demands. Perhaps that was the reason that it accepted extraordinary powers for the president in order to carry out economic reforms.

In order to ensure people's acceptance during the referendum what is required is availability of appropriate information to the people. This is more applicable in case of adoption of an important document like constitution for a country. It is also required that those who are going to take part in the referendum should be given sufficient time to go through the draft of the constitution. These conditions are the first steps towards ensuring transparency in the public affairs of a country's political system.

However, neither of these principles was followed during the constitution making procedures in Russia. The first meeting of the group was held on October 15, 1993 and the first draft of the new constitution was circulated on November 15, 1993 i.e., only four weeks before the constitutional referendum. Another decree on 15[h] October, 1993, stated that the constitution would be put to a vote of the people, which was subsequently held on 12 December. In a survey held before the referendum only 38 percent of

---

[14] See the interview of Sergei Filatov , Vice Chairman of CPD , *Izvestia, July 30, CDPSP, Vol XLIV, No. 30. 1992.* Filatov accused the ministers f or not coming to the parliament and sending their subordinates.

[15] See CDPSP Vol. XLIV. No. 45 (1992)

respondents claimed that they had read the draft.   [16] In other words, no transparent method was followed to ensure maximum participation of the voters.

In the referendum the Russian people were asked: 'Do you approve of the constitution of the Russian Federation'. A simple 'yes' or 'no' answer to this very general question was to determine the institutional framework for the legislature and executive branches; for the adoption of the December 1993 constitution, half of the electorate must vote and the majority of those voters must vote in favor of the constitution.

According to official statistics, 54.8 percent of the electorate voted; 58.4 percent of those voting (or 31 percent of the total electorate) supported the constitution; while 41.6 percent (or 22.1 percent of the electorate) voted against it. This is how the constitution was adopted. In fact the fairness of the referendum was also questioned. In a study published immediately after the December, 1993 it was shown that electoral fraud was very common in Russian regions. In many regions voter turnout was reported to be more than 99 percent. It is important to remember, that the referendum was held during the months of extreme winters in Russia. There were also reports of high percentage of disqualified ballots and lax monitoring by teams of international observers.

In another study Michael Urban has quoted an investigative study by a Special Expert Group appointed by theAdministration of the President to look into the electoral fraud. It reported that electoral turnout was not the 54.8 percent reported by the CEC but only 46.1 percent (Urban 1994: 133). In an explanatory note Troxel (2003, note 27: 207) refers to a study by the Centre for the Study of Public Policy/Paul Lazarsfeld Society (New Russia Barometer III, 94). This study questioned the Russian electorate as to who they thought should be more important in the Russian Federation, the president or the parliament, or should they have equal powers. The result was that 39 percent thought the president and parliament should be equal, 25 percent voted that

---

[16] Timothy Colton, "Public Opinion and the Constitutional R eferendum", in *Growing Pains: Russian Democracy and the Elections of 1993,*   Timothy Colton and Jerry Hough   *eds.* (Washington, D.C.: Brookings Institution Press, 1998), p. 293.

the president should be more important, and 22 percent believed parliament should be, while 13 percent were not sure.

On the basis of various statistical studies cited above, it can be said that the adoption of the constitution was the result of a manoeuvred and not participatory, accountable and transparent procedure. The constitution was neither a creation of constitutional convention nor of constituent assembly . Rather it was formulated by a narrow political clique appointed by the president. Commenting on the constitution making, Michael Urban argues, "One party to the year-long Constitutional crisis, headquartered in the Administration of the President, annulled the extant constitution, closed down legislative institutions, and designed a new governmental arrangement to ensure the future potential hegemony of those structures under its control" (Urban 1994: 134)

In addition to these tendencies of ignoring the public opinion or unwillingness to involve people in any form, there were hardly any attempts to create any political party . The Communist Party of Soviet Union was projected as the biggest threat and therefore banned. However   , the other groups were scattered in their orientation. There were attempts by these groups themselves to join hands. The president on the other hand never tried to bring all democratic forces together though always declared himself as the only guardian of democracy in the Russia. As a result, the emerging political groups could never get consolidated. Whenever there were attempts to bring these forces together, Yeltsin tried to make them divided by involving one section or the other in the government. [17]

An attempt to bring all opposition forces togethercreation of the National Salvation Front, was not allowed to function. It was immediately banned by the President Yeltsin by a decree. The Front was formed in order to oppose the president and his government.

Michael McFaul writes: "The new rules proposed in fall 1993 did not reflect the range of opinion on political and economic questions, nor did they emerge through compromise between elites. RatherYeltsin and his immediate

---

[17] "The Spectrum of Russia's (Proto) parties, CDPSP, Vol XLIV, No.33, 1992.

circle of advisors undertook an experiment in institutional design independent of other political actors and societal force" (McFaul: 2001: 209). It was not so that there was no possibility of reforms within the existing set up. In fact the opposition democratic forces time and again said that it should be done within the existing constitutional setup and use of force is also not desirable. But such voices were limited to media and people of Moscow . None of the policy makers, the parliament and the presidency gave adequate attention to such demands. [18]

II

DEATH OF PARTICIPATORY GOVERNANCE: ELECTORAL PROCEDURE

In the initial years political analysts questioned the relevance of elections in Russia.[19] Schmitter said that 'what definitely is not peculiar about Russia' s transition is the role that elections have (not) plated in it' (Schmitter 1993: 91). Since the adoption of a new constitution in 1993 Russia had experienced around eleven elections for the parliament and presidency apart from various regional elections. The election process has been regarded as largely free and fair and their outcomes are accepted by the political actors. The regime change has been taking place through the election procedures and not by use of violent techniques.

Elections under the new constitution

After some severe tensions between the between the executive and legislature in 1993, Russia adopted its new constitution. This constitution established a liberal democratic order along with guaranteeing civil liberties, a plural party system and free media. In other words, it fulfilled all the requirements which are considered necessary for a country to be considered as a democratic

---

[18] In an interview the Russian Democratic Reform Movement leade Gavriil Popov emphasized on this issue. See Izv estia July 31, 1992, *CDPSP, Vol XLIV, No. 31(1992).*

[19] Elections are r egarded as the most important pillars of a democr atic polit y. For few a democratic system is noting but election procedure. Bobbio says that, "..by democratic system I mean one in which supreme power (supreme in so far as it alone is authorized to use force as a last resort) is exerted in the name of and on behalf of the people by virtue of the procedure of elections" (quoted in Przeworski 1999).

polity. However, all these conditions have been fulfilled only on papers and no in reality. The procedure to electing the State Duma Deputies and Council of the Federation Members in December 1993 was established by a group of the Federation Members. It was headed by Duma Deputy Viktor Sheynis (Troxil 2003: 46). The 1993 Russian constitution established a four year term for Duma Deputies and the President, but the Council of Federation Members' terms were to be decided in their respective regions. Since the Council of the Federation is comprised of one executive head and one legislative leader from each of Russia's 89 regions, its members are not directly elected in federal elections but are elected in regional elections; with the regional legislature deciding what positions will represent the region in the council.

For the State Duma a mixed electoral system was adopted. One half of the seats (225) are allocated through registered parties' lists on a proportional basis of the votes that the party receives in elections, as long as the party obtains at least 5 percent of the vote. The other half (225) of deputies are selected from a plurality vote in single-member constituencies.Adoption of a mixed electoral system was nothing but to ensure strong position for the president himself. Michael Urban calls the institution making in Russia as "democracy by design" where "those in control of the state machinery attempt to shape the institutions and procedures of a competitive election on ways that ensure an electoral outcome favorable to the designers themselves."

Electoral frauds in Russian elections

On the basis of regularity of elections many scholars have concluded that Russian democracy is moving towards stabilization.   Valerie Bunce (2003: 182-83) argues: "Since independence, Russia has held five elections at the national level-and hundreds more at the regional level. These elections have by and large been free and fair". Similarly MacFaul writes that Russian democracy has successfully institutionalized elections (McFaul and Petrov: 2004).

Studies in the recent past have shown that there is a clear linkage between the way citizens perceive elections –fair or unfair (Birch 2005) Fabrice Lehoucq (2002: 35) argues: "electoral fraud undermines citizens' ability to constrain the action of state officials…to the extent that public officials can corrupt the electoral process, they are less accountable to the electorate."

In 1993 first elections were held under the provisions of the new constitution. A large number of groups participated in these elections. A representation threshold was incorporated into the party-list system to prevent the proliferation of small parties. For entry into the parliament a party had to take at least 5 percent of the national vote, with the whole country was considered as one constituency .

Candidates required a minimum of one percent nomination to enter the contest in single-member districts unless they had been nominated officially by one of the party blocs in which case the necessity of obtaining what on average was 4–5000 signatures was relaxed. The other 225 seats in the State Duma were distributed to the parties on a proportional basis as long as they cleared the 5 percent threshold.

However, Steven Fish argues that "falsification, coercion, and the arbitrary disqualification of candidates in elections, as well as construction of communicative interaction and associational life, have prevented democracy from taking hold" (Fish 2005: 29). While using Dahl's criteria of measuring free and fair elections he has shown how elections in Russia does not fulfill the criteria of free and fair election system.

Fish argues that electoral fraud is a normal phenomenon in Russian elections. Tempering with the numbering of vote polled in favor of a candidate is the most regular fraud. Election related coercions are also frequent. Administrative resources have been misused by the candidates who are already in the power structure or have some links in the administration. Candidates have been excluded from taking part in the elections. Besides, Fish also shows how civil liberties, which are considered necessary for free expression of people's will, have been restricted by various means. Candidates are not allowed to communicate with the citizens freely and there are limitations on association of the people.

Before the 1993 elections, thirty-one associations scrambled to form electoral blocs in time for the deadline, and twenty-one sought to find the required list of nominations. There were allegations that the authorities disturbed the signature campaign, and the police detained oppositional activists and confiscated the signatures that they managed to collect.

Like all national elections in Russia, each of the country's 94,864 voting precincts writes an official document, called a protocol, which records the results. The precincts tally the votes immediately after the polls close (usually at 8pm), record them in the form of the protocols, and send their protocols up to the territorial electoral commissions, which number several hundred. Territorial commissions send their tallies to the regional electoral commissions, one of which is located in each of Russia' s 89 provinces. The regional commissions then report their results to the federal Central Electoral Commission (CEC) in Moscow.

Reporters from the *Moscow Times*, who conducted a major investigation of the 2000 election, managed to obtain 245 of Dagestan' s 1,550 protocols. Comparing the protocols that they were able to obtain with the territorial commission's reported totals the *Times* found 87, 139 fewer votes for Putin in the former than appeared in the later (Fish 2005: 34).

The votes cast in these 245 provinces accounted for 16 percent of Dagestan's precincts. If the rate of over reporting for Putin in the 84 percent of the precincts that the investigators did not have access to was the same as it was I the 16 percent on which they did manage to gather data, 551,287 votes of the 877,853 that Putin officially won in Dagestan would have been attributed to him wrongly.

Election results for the elections for State Duma

Party	2007		2003	
	Number of seats	Vote received (Percent)	Number of seats	Vote received (Percent)
United Russia	315	64.3	222	37.6
Communist Party of Russian Federation	57	11.6	52	12.6
Liberal democratic party of Russia	40	8.1	36	11.5
Just Russia	38	7.7	-	-

Source: Central Election Commission of Russia website

Table 3.1

The *Times* investigators found discrepancies in other places in which it was able to obtain protocols as well. In Saratov' s polling precinct number 1,617, the original precinct results as recorded in the protocols gave Putin 666 votes; the results reported by the territorial commission gave him 1,086. in precinct number 1,797 the analogus figures were 667 and 995, in precinct number 1,591 they were 822 and 1,012 (Borisova 2000, Fish 2003: 35) .

It is really hard to obtain the protocols from the officials. Even the higher officials do not pressurize the lower officials to make them available as the case in other democracies.

Furthermore, the Central Election Commission (CEC)' s reporting of results on election night provides grounds for further speculation about what happens to votes as they move up the hierarchy of electoral commissions. According to the CEC, as of 6 pm, 59.2 percent of Dagestan' s registered voters had cast their ballots. By the close of voting at 8 pm, however , that number had sur ged to 83.6 percent. A sociologist who examined the data noted of the reporting: 'Normally most people come in the morning, then attendance decreases slowly and in the end, there is a small rise, but not a vertical skyrocket of visitors'(Fish 2006: 35).According to the analyst 'ghost voters' or 'dead souls' created by electoral commissions almost certainly accounted for a large portion of the voters in Dagestan who allegedly rushed to the polls in the closing two hours of voting. It is quite easy to find a clear impact of presidentialism on the electoral performances in Russian polity (Moser 1998: 54-75).

In its report *Nations in Transit,* the Freedom House has also rated Russia in the category of states with poor performance in electoral procedure (See Table 3.1). This analysis is based on 1-7 scale. Here 1 indicates as the best performance in the field of electoral laws and fairness in electoral procedures, whereas 7 is the poorest performance on the scale.

A close analysis of the table explains how Russia since 1997 has never been close to the best performance point. Rather its performance has gone down since last decade. In the year 2007 it was at 6.25. On the other hand the neighboring East-European democracies have been performing well. All the countries who were part of the former Soviet Union are poor performers in terms of electoral procedures.

Electoral Process Fairness: Russia and other neighboring countries

	2001	2002	2003	2004	2005	2006	2007	2008	2009	2010
Russia	4.25	4.5	4.75	5.5	6	6.25	6.5	6.75	6.75	6.75
Kazakhstan	6.25	6.25	6.5	6.5	6.5	6.5	6.5	6.75	6.75	6.75
Kyrgyzstan	5.75	5.75	6	6	6	5.75	5.75	6	6	6.25
Polad	1.25	1.25	1.5	1.5	1.75	1.75	2	2	2	1.75

Source: Freedom House Reports Nations in Transit (2007) available at www.freedomhouse.org

Table 3.2
Electoral Process
Ratings History and Regional Breakdown

NOTES: The ratings are based on a scale of 1 to 7, with 1 representing the highest level of democratic progress and 7 the lowest. The 2006 ratings reflect the period January 1 through December 31, 2005.

Negative consequences of an unfair election procedure are very much evident from the election outcomes. Parties which enjoy support of the presidential administration are the winners. Various surveys express people's dissatisfaction with the existing system. The chart shows how people distrust the institutions which are the product of elections. In a survey only 36 percent of people said that they trust the Duma members. Only twenty nine percent citizens trust political parties.

A report of Radio Free Europe reported in 2002 that during 2001 and 2002, governors Sergei Darkin of primorskii krai and Boris Govorin of Irkutsk oblast and President Valerii Kokov of Kabardino-Balkar autonomous republic, were three examples, who regularly sent the police to the vendors to confiscate and destroy runs of the one or handful of newspapers left in their bailiwicks that publishes unflattering articles.

Conclusion

As a result of these tendencies people have lost faith in two of the most significant institutions of democracy building, one the constitution and second elections. This has been the reason that on the one hand the voting percentage has been declining. On the other hand there are continues reports of violations of various constitutional provisions by the regions of Russian federation. Despite various attempts by Putin and now by Medvedev such instances are continue to rise. This has resulted into the weakness of Russian state in ensuring an effective implementation of its own public policies as we shall see in the next chapters.

Chapter Four

Ensuring Participation:
Institutions and Governance in Russia

Adopting a representative democracy based on a multi-party system was a clear departure from the Marxist ideology based political system to a liberal ideology. In the Marxist ideology there is no space for rival ideological factions. Only the organizations which adhere to the Marxian ideas of society, politics and economy are allowed to function. In the liberal ideology on the other hand even rival, or what Sartori calls 'anti system parties' are also allowed to function. In other words, there is a scope for participation of the section which may not agree with the existing set of institutions and principles.

In case of post-Soviet Russia, elections for presidency and parliament on the basis of multi party system was a step forward in developing a more liberal state. However, a closer look at the performance of these institutions and their comparison with the other countries undergoing transition shows that these institutions are neither based on fair procedures nor they are truly representative in their nature.

After adoption of procedures of democratic polity the second crucial step towards democratization is establishing institutions which support democratic practice. Institutions are associations or set of rules or norms. Institutions are also defined as: 'constraints that shape behavior in various areas of human activity; stretching from social interaction to economic exchange to international cooperation' (MacIntyre 2003: 3).

Theories of participation look at the institutions and their ability to ensure participation of various sections in the political system. In the governance literature these institutions are analysed in terms of their fairness, and transparency in their functioning. These institutions are the foremost pillars of making a political system representative. They also ensure a stronger link between the state on the one hand and society on the other .

While studying the participation and decentralization aspect of institutions, MacIntyre in his study of four South-East   Asian countries has shown how the great economic breakdown restructured their political institutions in order to revive their economies. He argues that the level of fragmentation of decision-making power, i.e. participation aspect of good governance, among various institutions affects the nature, speed and implementation of the decisions taken. The more power is fragmented, the greater are the problems in decision-making. On the other hand, a centralized institutional political structure suffers from the problems of imposition of decisions. He has (see Figure 4.1) shown that higher polarization of power (on both ends- highly decentralized and centralized) affects the decision-making negatively . Countries having institutions with appropriate checks and balances and establishing a balance between the two poles have effective decision-making process.

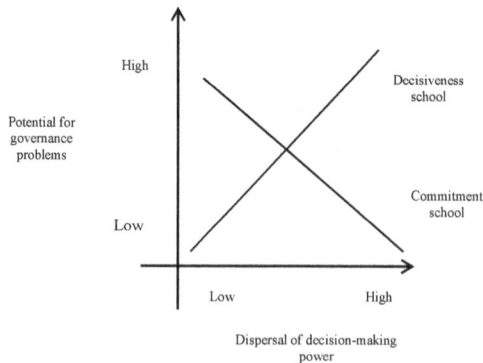

Figure 4.1
The interrelationship between the concentrations of
Decision-making power and effectiveness of institutions
Source: MacIntyre 2001: 6

Institutions which connect state with the society play very significant role in the transition polities. Some such institutions are: the government, political parties, civil society and bureaucracy . Government consists of legislature, executive and judiciary. Political parties are the mechanisms by which people convert their demands to the government. Civil society is the informal network between the state and society . Bureaucracy is responsible for implementation of government policies. Success or failure of state policies largely depends on the efficiency of bureaucratic system.

In post-Soviet Russia, presidency has been assigned highly significant role in determining the governance principles of the country . The 1993 constitution gives primacy to the president over all other political institutions. As discussed in the previous chapter the Russian president played the most significant role in determining the constitutional framework of the country . Consequently development of other political institutions depends on their relationship with the presidency . Although political parties are allowed to function independently and a bicameral legislature has also been established, the president has emerged as the supreme policy-maker Similarly the evolution of civil society has been hampered by the concentration of powers in the hands of the presidency. Various civil society institutions such media, interest groups, or the non-governmental organizations are allowed to function only if their position is not adversarial to the Russian presidentAll these institutions have faced serious threat to their existence if they stood against the presidency

In fact the Russian president has emer ged as a strong national leader . Keeping in view all these developments this study hypothesizes thata strong presidential regime dominates other political institutions (parliament and civil society) in Russia, leading to centralized governance, and finally a weak and centralized state. (See Table 4.1)

In order to study impact of presidency the study selects its relationship with the parliament, civil society and the Russian bureaucracy . This chapter argues that in the institutional sphere basic principles of democratic governance have been ignored so that all other institutions depend on the presidency for performing their functions. An efficient and strong civil society could play the role of catalyst in the democratization process and make the state more decentralized and accountable to people only if it has some role to play in the decision-making process. Such a state will all have more legitimacy as compared to a state which rests upon the bureaucracy for its interaction with the society. Similarly a strong parliament keeps checks on the executive' s actions. The parliament is the supreme legislation making body . It drafts, discusses, and adopts laws. It represents people' s voice. It also provides political parties scope to influence decision-making.

In the post-Soviet Russia the presidency and not the parliament determines basic guidelines of the policy-formation. The new constitution categorically assigns these responsibilities to the president. President has been vested with extraordinary powers to ensure stability of the political system. Parliament is considered as a source of instability and therefore causing weak state.

Independent variables — Institutions	Constitutional Powers	Role in the Government formation	Role in the Policy-format-ion	Level of trust among the people
Presidency	Dominant	Dominant	Dominant	Maximum
Parliament: State Duma and Federation Council	Less as compared to the president	Less as compared to government formation	Depends on the cooperation with the president	Less as compared to the president
Civil society	No such powers	Weak	Weak	Very less
Political parties	Powers to function independently	Weak	Weak	Less

Table 4.1
Comparison of various institutions in terms of their constitutional powers,
their role in the government formation and policy making

Various comparative studies have shown how a strong parliament and not the presidency or executive system makes the system less corrupt.   A strong presidency leads to patronage politics and concentrates power in the hands of few. In order to achieve good governance and an ef fective state —

corruption, patronage politics and centralization of power— need to be checked. A presidential system with weak political parties and not having any history of democratic movements stimulates and not controls these evils. The following discussion tries to show the link between emergence of strong presidency, corruption and weakening of other institutions, and emer gence of a weak state as their collective effect.

I

THE RUSSIAN PARLIAMENT

Various democratization and governance studies have shown that a strong parliament helps in achieving good governance. A major step towards establishing a democratic polity in new Russia was establishing multi-party system and a Parliament where these parties can influence the process of decision-making. The Russian Constitution provides a bicameral legislature. The lower house is called the State Duma whereas the upper house is known as the Federation Council. The State Duma is the main decision-making body as the Constitution states that the council only functions on a part-time basis. This does not mean that the Council of Federation is power-less, but only that its power in the decision-making is much more limited than the Duma' s by the infrequency of sessions and in the policy areas of laws it can approve.

Steven Fish *et al* (2003) have developed a Parliamentary Power Index (PPI) to measure the strength of a parliament in any country . The PPI is based on various powers of the parliament enshrined by the constitution as well as in real polity . The Parliamentary Power Index shows that greater parliamentary powers lead to an open polity and less corruption. (see Table 4.2)

However, in a cross-country analysis of post-Soviet states Fish ar gues that "what matters for democracy is the strength of the legislature, rather than whether the constitutional system is formally presidential, parliamentary or semi-presidential. Countries with more potent parliaments have done better than those with weaker parliaments". (Fish 2005: 209). It is based on around eighty independent variables which determine the degree of powers of the parliament. The PPI focuses more on the constitutional powers given to the parliament.

However, the governance analysis, apart from constitutional provisions for the parliament, also includes extra-constitutional variables. It also takes into account a parliament's efficiency, accountability, level of transparency and its ability to keep an eye on other institutions. A comparative analysis of both the methods (see   Table 4.3) explains that a political system –with a strong parliament along with accountability and responsiveness to the voters' demands, provides better governance as compare to the countries with strong presidential regimes and weak parliaments.

Country	PPI	Country	PPI
Albania	.75	Lithuania	.72
Armenia	.53	Macedonia	.78
Azerbaijan	.44	Moldova	.72
Belarus	.28	Mongolia	.81
Bulgaria	.78	Poland	.66
Croatia	.72	Romania	.72
Czech republic	.78	Russia	.44
Estonia	.75	Slovakia	.72
Georgia	.59	Slovenia	.78
Hungary	.69	Tajikistan	.41
Kazakhstan	.31	Ukraine	.50
Kyrgyzstan	.41	Uzbekistan	.28
Latvia	.84		

Table 4.2
Parliamentary Power Index Scores
Source: Fish 2005: 206 [1]

A comparison between the Parliamentary Power Index and   World Governance Survey shows the relationship between the powers and effectiveness of parliament and condition of governance in a country.Mongolia with maximum score in the list of compared countries scores also provides highest score in the governance index. Similarly Bulgaria with second rank in terms of parliamentary power scored second in theWorld Governance Survey.

Countries	PPI	WGS
Bulgaria	0.78	83
Kyrgyzstan	0.41	75
Mongolia	0.81	86
Russia	0.44	73

Table 4.3
Comparison of PPI and WGS

Various studies ar gue that countries under going transition with strong Parliaments have moved faster on the path of democratization rather than countries with strong Presidential systems. The strength of Parliament also depends on its organization. David Olson and Philip Norton maintain that:

'the extent to which a legislature is well organized and well equipped can affect its ability to participate in the policy process…If it has some latitude for independent thought and action, its ability to take advantage of those opportunities is affected by the extent to which it is internally organized. The main means by which legislatures are internally organized are political parties and committees. Parties in democratic legislatures are usually few in number , lar ge in size, and relatively 'strong' while committees tend to be more numerous smaller in size and "week" ' (Olson and Norton 1996: 9).

In Russia the presidential powers have encroached on the parliamentary powers. The new Constitution gives power to issue decree to the President in case of emer gency. So far this power had been misused by the President to by pass the parliament. Other studies of institutions in the Russia, (Remington 2001), however, do not concur with this notion.   With the help of various empirical explanations these studies have shown that in spite of weak and fragmented party system Russian Parliament has influenced the process of policy formation. Though its effectiveness is less as compared to many Parliaments in the developed world yet it is not a completely marginalized institution.

During initial Yeltsin period Parliament influenced the process of policy formulation and law making. The politics in Russia during this period was marked by confrontation between the president and the parliament. However despite these the first Duma in 1994 produced a considerable number of legislations; during the Second Duma (1996-99) 500 bills were passed and signed into law by the president.

In the law making field, president enjoys the power to veto the legislation passed by the Parliament whereas the Parliament (the State Duma and The Federation Council) can also veto the Presidential legislation. However the powers of President depend on number of factors. Primarily his association with any party and the strength of that party in the Parliament (the State Duma) is the most significant factor The confrontation between the legislature and executive was at its peak during the first five-six years after adoption of the new Constitution. It was so because during this period communists and the ultra-nationalist parties were in power . The parties which were favoring Yeltsin were on the margins. Consequently Parliament and President were in a conflict situation on many issues especially on the issue of appointment of Prime Minister, passing the budget and removal of minister.

To a great extent Parliamentary efficiency depends on the efficiency of parties in the political system. As argued before, political parties in Russian federation are weak. Apart from existence of strong presidency their own organizational weaknesses have made them ineffective. Change of party by the State Duma deputies in the first two Duma tenures was one such example. Besides, parties have very less role to play in the selection of president, prime minister and his cabinet. Rather it is the president whose opinion dominates over others. In other words, existence of party depends on the party rather than the party affecting the president.

These trends have more or less continued during Putin's presidency and even after wards. However, the confrontational politics has came to an end. Putin has successfully managed a 'cooperative parliament' which was being dominated by the members of his party of favor- the United Russia. The opposition is rather divided and more or less supportive of Putin and the President, supported by him.

II

POLITICAL PARTIES AND PARTY SYSTEM

Parties are the mechanisms through which people communicate their demands to the government. In the modern era of democratization, they are considered most important component for the effective functioning of democracy. They provide representation, form and recruit elites, determine goals of the political system, articulate the interests of citizens, and ensure political socialization.

Besides, in understanding governance and nature of any political system what are important are the way political parties function and their effectiveness in the polity. Effectiveness here means the role parties play in government formation and decision-making process. Their significance in these procedures makes them relevant in any political system (Sartori 1966: 75). According to Richard Rose and Neil Munro (2002: 101) parties can provide democratic government only if their outcome decides collective control of decision-making in government. They identify four requirements in order to make a collective decision making by parties. Firstly, political elites or ganize parties to fight elections rather than appeal for votes as personalities independent of parties. Secondly, parties must nominate candidates nationwide.Third, national party candidate rather than independent candidates, local parties or separatist regional parties should win the great majority of votes and seats.A fourth requirement is that parties nominate candidates for all elected national offices – is most readily met in a British style parliamentary government, where a single ballot decides which party has a majority and therefore names the prime minister . Fifth and finally, for a majority of voters to hold governors accountable for their behaviour in office, parties should persist from one election to another. If a party system fulfills these requirements than there are higher possibilities of keeping a government accountable which further ensures good governance.

Richard Sakwa (1995: 91) identifies four features of the political parties in new Russia: emphasis on personalities; amorphous and poorly drafted programmes, the deinstitutionalizing influence of regional politics; the constant splitting and sub-dividing of parties and factions; and the absence of party discipline. These features are quite opposite to the requirements identified by Neil Munro and Richard Rose.

The Russian party system is characterized by differences resulting in variety of functional behaviour of parties. Rose and Munro describe Russian party system as "four systems (italics in original) of parties" rather than a multi-party system or a four party system. In other words parties behave in different ways.

The independent candidates far outnumber party standard-bearers. They have been winning most votes and seats and not the parties. Besides, there is a big disjunction between the electoral parties and Duma parties. Parties do not persist in the subsequent elections. Most Russian parties are 'ephemeral'. Finally, explaining the social base of political parties Sakwa further asserts that the absence of a recognizable social base to the new political parties was perhaps the single most important factor inhibiting the development of party politics (Sakwa 1996: 95).

If a country does not have independent, free and fair election process parties will not be effective. In case of Russia, as explained earlier, elections are not free and fair (Fish 2005). There are examples of manipulation and fraud in elections. Among such circumstances it is not easy for the parties to be an effective player in the political system. There are number of factors which have resulted in such developments in Russia.

Besides parties are not free from the influence of Russian oligarchs. (For details see chapter five) They are funded by corporate group. Consequently the parties' agenda is nothing but the agenda of the company which supports it. Companies have been sponsoring presidential candidates as well. This trend became stronger after 1995, but following the 1998 crisis funding has reduced drastically. Gazprom, the oil giant was the main sponsor of Our Home is Russia, and later on provided generous support to Unity and still later to the United Russia, a group that was also funded by Lukoil, Sibneft and Russian Aluminium. Fatherland had been financed by Moscow financial groups beholden to Luzhkov, while All Russia and the Russiaś Regions group of deputies were supported by Lukoil, Interos, and the regional oil companies Tatneft and Bashneft. The opposition liberal party Yabloko had been supported by Gusinsky's Most group from its earliest days in 1993, not only with funds but with favorable coverage and access to NTV.Later Yabloko's main sponsor became Yukos, headed by Khodorkovsky (which also supported SPS and CPRF).

The other main liberal grouping, the Union of Right Forces (SPS) was financed by Yukos, Alfa-TNK and Chubais UES, and in general the party was tainted by its perhaps excessively close oligarchical connections. On the left the CPRF and the Agrarian Party have been funded by various branches of the military –industrial complex and the engineering industry , in particular Rosagropromstroi headed by the 'red-director ' Victor Vidamov, who since 1998 has had a seat on the CPRF' s presidium.

Apart from funding parties, some of the giant state monopolies such as Gazprom, UES and the railway ministry have been very active in supporting candidates in single-mandate constituencies. In the 1999 elections Gazprom supported some 130 candidates and provided them with specialist electoral advice from one of the leading political consultancy firms, Niccolo-M. [1]

Discussing the reasons behind such a relationship between the party and business groups Richard Sakwa argues that these are attempts to "advance

---

[1] During the filed work I interviewed many experts and students of political science in the Moscow State Univ ersity. Most of them agr eed that the agenda of an y poli tical party is determined by the company which f unds that part y. For mor e details on this also see Sakwa 2004: 200.

the Kremlin's 'parties of power ' and the election of presidents, and this in turn was seen as a way of protecting their gains and interests. As a result of this nexus parties are not the mouthpiece of people but spokesperson of oligarchs. Putin made attempts to evolve an alternative national based party. To some extent these attempts have been successful but have failed to fully control the role of oligarchs in the party politics.

In addition to the business-party nexus what has affected the development of an effective party system is the institutional structure (MacFaul 2001). Legislatures are the platform where parties, either as a ruling party or as an opposition, put people' s demands before the government.   The Russian Parliament is not as strong institution as it is in other democratic countries. Though parties are allowed to perform many important functions in the law making process but due to the emerging nature of polity the parties are not independent and significant players.

Besides, parties are organizationally weak institutions and their presence is limited to the urban areas. Only Communist Party has a nationwide presence due to its strong organizational infrastructure which was built during the Soviet period. Existence of all other parties is dependent on their leader and not on their performance in elections.

In addition to these weaknesses, the performance of parties has not been very impressive. The manifesto on which they fiught the elections gets diluted after the elections. This has reduced their credibilityamong the Russians. Their changing stance on various national issues has negatively affected their image. Parties have been unable to provide any effective program to the voters. Consequently their role has been weak and the President' s role continues to grow.

Deputies have been changing their parties so frequently that there is no accountability and commitment for a party-ideology In a study Stephen White has shown that these change in commitments leave voter confused about the agenda for which they elected the candidate. This has further reduced the faith of voters in the parties.

Besides, except the Communist Party of Russian Federation (CPRF) and now the United Russia, no other party has a nationwide presence. In fact, parties are more interested in the middle-class urban voters rather than appealing to rural voters. Communist party has an existence since the Soviet days which provides it an advantage over other parties. This limited presence is also reflected from the number of candidates which parties nominate from various areas. Apart from the Communist Party no other party had given tickets to candidates from all over the country .

There are examples which show that executive-legislature relations are shifting from 'confrontation to cooperation' (Troxel 2003:3). There have been examples where the Parliament influenced the policy agenda of the government. This has been due to number of reasons. After experience of a decade now the Parliament as well as the President seems to realize the importance of negotiation among the key government institutions. It was evident during Yeltsin's period that a hostile Duma would be a danger for the stability of the nation. Even the Parliament realizes that confrontation with the President harms their image among the people.

Although political parties remain week but Putin after taking over as the President cleverly ensured a Parliament of his own supporters. Instead of marginalizing Parliament Putin himself has joined a political party called United Russia. During last two elections the United Russia got absolute majority in the lower house of the Parliament.This was due to Putin's popularity and his association with the party.

A study by Troxel shows that the decrees issued by the President were non-normative in nature. These decrees were not related to major policy areas. In her analysis she has explained how the normative decrees have been issued by President. Parliament also consulted on important policy issues. Another factor which has strengthened role of the parliament in the law making process is representation of political parties in the parliamentary committees. These committees are responsible for preparing the draft of law and for other financial matters.

III

CIVIL SOCIETY, GOVERNANCE, AND THE STATE

Etymologically, the word civil society (*societas civilis*) is 'derived by pre-modern Europeans from Cicero's definition of the state (*ivitas*) as a partnership in law (*societies*) with equality of legal status, but not of money and talent, among its members' (Black 2002: 33). Later on, it became a generic term for a secular legal and political order as distinct from a primitive society.

Civil society has at least three key roles to perform. Firstly, it socializes the masses, makes them aware of their political rights and obligations and promotes them as active players in the political life of the country. Secondly, it fosters associational growth. It brings more organized forms of collective life where people can sit together and discuss issues of social significance. Finally, it creates an enabling environment for policy inputs. It is this factor which makes the study of civil society significant for the process of democratization in the post-Soviet countries. The more civil society networks are involved in the decision-making process, the more the possibilities of better implementation of various governmental policies. This study includes modern institutions of civil society such as the media (print and electronic), and various non-governmental organizations.

A popular perception is that the Russian state has been a stumbling block in the evolution of a free civil society , as it has been authoritarian in nature throughout the history. During the Soviet period, especially during Stalin' s period no civil society was allowed to flourish outside of party defined limits. This feature led to characterization of Soviet state as a totalitarian state.

However, various studies (Whittaker 1984, Lincoln 1990, and Conroy 1976) argue that, a tentative civil society was visible in imperial Russia at least from the late eighteenth century though it really expanded in the second half of the nineteenth and early twentieth centuries. Conroy's study is full of evidences on how civil society institutions flourished during the imperial Russia (Conroy 2006).

A combination of government policies and private initiatives helped in increasing the level of education and created an environment conducive for the high public participation in policy making. These efforts were not merely government initiatives. Private organizations played a key role in developing social networks.

However, such developments got discontinued during the Soviet era. There are various streams of thought about civil society evolution in Soviet Russia. Some scholars believe that Soviet state's mechanisms were so pervasive that there were no independent social organizations (Biddulph 1975; Pavlova 1998). This school also believes that Soviet citizens were completely subjugated to direction by the political regime.

Another school believes that by the late 1980s, an embryonic civil society had taken shape in the Soviet Union (White 1999). Many scholars argue that the main ideology of Soviet state was to accomplish economic development and social security . Perhaps it was assumed that modernization will automatically lead to independent evolution of civil society (Evans 2006: 28-54). During this period only those organizations which were functioning within the limits of Communist party were allowed.

There are some studies which do not agree with the notion that autonomy was fully absent from Soviet society Studies by Millar (1987a) and Zimmerman (1987) are among them. They believe that there is strong empirical basis to believe that the informal connections and tradeoffs that were used by Soviet citizens to make the system work for them became more important from one generation to another in the post-Stalin period. This school of thought argues that the Soviet society was not entirely passive in its reaction to initiatives undertaken by the political regime, even after the full consolidation of Stalinism. People in the USSR were not independent who obediently followed all directions from the state and internalized all the party's values and goals as their own.

The civil society in post-Soviet Russia has also been facing challenges from the state.Although when a new Constitution came in place, it guaranteed the freedom of media and freedom of expression, the trends since 1991 have however not always been supportive for the evolution of a vibrant civil society

The following discussion discusses various aspects of civil society development in Russia:

Media

Channel	Name	Ownership	Daily reach(percent)
1	Russian ublicP television (ORT)	51 percent owned by the state, the rest by a mix of public and private corporations	84
2	Russian Televisiona nd Radio (RTR)	100 percent state-owned	71
3	TV-Centre	Funded primarily by the city of Moscow	16
4	NTV	Commercial but now controlled by state interests	53
5	Culture	State-owned; cultural channel created by Presidential decree in 1997. Only television channel not to carry paid advertising	8
6	Sports channel TVS (Formerly TV-6)	Commercial. Formerly TVS or TV-6 commercial channel. Inherited NTV news team when NTV taken over by state interests, but was then itself closed for alleged fiscal mismanagement in 2003	NA

Table 4.4

National Television Channels in Russia

Source is Oates 2006: 65

Despite a brief period of autonomy at the end of the Soviet regime, the Russian media remained polarized between various political views. Rather than becoming an arena for free expression and discussion, it had become a tool in the hands of ruling regime. During the transition, as the Presidential administration and the business elite consolidated their power, the media has become less open and much less free. Particularly on the state-run television, the most popular medium in the country , there is little unbiased political information for viewers.

Russia has all the technical infrastructure necessary for the development of a modern civil society. There are prominent state run media, including the flagship Russian Public Television (Obshchestvennoe rossiiskoe televidenie or ORT). There is a wide range of state-run and commercial television stations across the vast country. (see Table 4.4) There are several major newspapers and wealth of specialty publications. There are both state and commercial radio stations. The Internet, albeit currently with low usage, is growing rapidly and features many news, politics, and entertainment sites.

However, presence of these mediums of communication does not make the evolution of civil society an easy going af   fair. While the new Russian Constitution of 1993 contains guarantees regarding freedom of information and the banning of censorship, the period from 1991 to 1993 can best be described as a time of benign neglect of the mass media.

The initial years of post-Communist Russia were years of relatively more openness for media.Although President Yeltsin objected to many of the reports on him in the mass media on the whole he did not broadly impose controls or pressure the mass media with dubious legal maneuvers (aside from briefly banning the media that supported the reactionary Parliament).

However, government and establishment friendly behavior of Russian media was exposed during and after the 1993 Parliamentary elections. Russia passed a liberal campaign law, allowing parties and candidates free and equal access to state-run television and newspapers. Most of the campaigning focused on the race for the lower house of the Russian Parliament, the 450-seat Duma. The campaign rules included an hour of free broadcast time for all thirteen parties in the election, as well as free space in major newspapers to campaign. In addition, parties and candidates were allowed to buy paid advertising, even on the television.   Technically constrained by campaign spending limits, the financial rules were largely ignored. Several parties, including the pro-government Russia' s Choice and nationalist Liberal-Democrats, bought paid advertising space on a large scale.

Although the campaign law called for fair and equal coverage of political parties, Russia's Choice received an excessive amount of coverage on *Vermya* while the Communist Party of the Russian Federation received no coverage (Oates 1998). During the 1993 campaign, journalists generally ignored the flamboyant nationalist Vladimir Zhirinovsky, who made several xenophobic and racist comments during his free time speeches and paid advertising.

These instances between the party-of-power and the other non-ruling parties have continued even in the subsequent election campaigns for the Parliament (1995, 1999 and 2003). It was described broadly as unfair in three ways. First, pro-government parties and candidates- even those with little voter appeal- continued to receive an inordinate amount of coverage. Second, the Communists and others, seen as a challenge to the Russian government, received substantially less coverage, and often it was less than positive. For example, an analysis of news content on ORT and NTV in the 1999 campaign found that the Communists received just 5 percent of the election news coverage on ORT, and just 3 percent of the election news coverage on NTV-despite winning the large number of votes in the Duma party-list contest. In addition, by 1999 journalist were practicing the dubious tactics of 'black propaganda', smearing candidates with scandal-laden stories with little journalistic integrity, and not allowing for a proper reply from the victims.

It is important to mention that the entire media in Russia is not run by the state. There is a sizeable private media industry , although the last national commercial television station that openly opposed the Putin regime was taken off the air in 2003.[2] Although private media has worked against a government monopoly on information, the structure of the media environment in Russia has militated against those efforts. Many experts on media believe that the commercial media are critical to maintaining a balance of information. In this way, commercial media has a particular advantage over the state-run media, a critical ability to criticize without the fear of retaliation from political patrons.

Putin was determined to strengthen the Russian state and enhance Russia' status as a respected power , and that he regarded economic growth and

---

[2] For more detail on this issue see a report on Internews at www.internews.ru/en/rumedia/ 2003

internal order as necessary means to those ends. [3] Putin's style to implement his plans cautiously and gradually often using indirect methods of discouraging independent criticism, while ostensibly endorsing democracy and the rule of law, are nevertheless not favorable for development of independent media.[4]

There has been intense debate over the nature of Russian state after Vladimir Putin became the President of Russia. In the words of Michael McFaul (2004), "Putin has undermined every independent source of political power in Russia during the past few years."

Initially, some analysts invented terms such as "managed democracy" or "virtual democracy" to explain the complexity of Putin' s design. Gordon Hahn's (2004) description of Putins 'stealth authoritarianism' or Aleksei Zudin's (2003) concept of Putin' s 'monocentrism' seem to be more accurate portrayals. The real question is no longer whether Putin wants to decrease the degree of pluralism in the Russian polity, or whether he can successfully manipulate political forces to make that possible [5], since the answers to both these questions are obviously affirmative; the real challenge for researchers is to discern the contours of the structures that Putin sought to construct.

Russia's small group of financial houses and oil and gas companies gobbled up many of Russia' s national news papers. Opposition publications such as *Zavtra, Sovetskaya Rossiya,* and the dozens of publications put out by the Liberal Democratic Party of Russia have survived the transition to the market economy, but their circulations are small. Regional newspapers still remain

---

[3] On various occasions President Putin immediate and great need of a strong state. For his various addressed see "Russia: Putin Comes on Str ong", available at RFE/ RL Newsline onhttp://www.rferl.org/featuresarticle/2007/02/a66a3010-27ac-4a85-b74f-1fd6eaa0d210.html, and "Putin Advocates Some State R egulation of Economy, But Not Too Much", *Inter fax News Agency, Moscow,* SWB SU/3777 B/1, 1 March 2000. Also see "Putin Calls for Consistency Between Regional, Federal Laws", *Inter fax News Agency,* 22 March 2000, SWB SU/3797 B/1, 24 March 2000, "Putin T urns Out T o Be A R adical", *Nezavisimaya Gazeta,* March 31, 2000, p.3, *CDPSP,* Vol. 52, No. 13, April 26, 2000, p. 6.

[4] "Puitn Says Strong State Means Effective Russia", *Inter fax News Agency,* 31 March 2000, SWB SU/3805 B/1, 3 April 2000.

[5] "Putin Proposes Major R evamping of Senate- Vladimir Putin-Government Has to W ork!", *Rossiiskaya Gazeta,* May 19, 2000, p .3, *CDPSP,* Vol. 52, No. 20, June 14 , 2000, p. 4 .

independent from Moscow' s oligarchs, but they are tied closely to local governors.

The nature of Russia' s transition from communist rule allowed for an explosion of new sources of information and a vibrant independent media. On the whole, the Russian print media or press still remain free of state control and provides a wide spectrum of viewsAt the same time, the continued role of the state in owning and managing media resources, particularly the national television networks, has weakened this important democratic institution in the last one decade.A more successful market reform might have produced a more independent media.

Non-governmental organizations

Non-governmental organizations are those organizations which work for various public issues but they do not come under the government'jurisdiction as a formal governmental agency Their nature of work and area difer widely. Here the status of trade union and human rights groups is discussed.

In the post-Soviet Russia west sponsored NGOs have been mushrooming. They are active in poverty reduction programmes, human right awareness, in the field of education and fight against corruption. Howeverafter the colored revolutions in the neighboring countries, Russian government decided to keep a check on the NGO activities and their funding sources. In order to do so a new NGO law was passed. This law was criticized by many western scholars as an attack on the civil society development in Russia.

In order to gain some popularity and to bring NGOs with the government the Kremlin organized a meet of NGOs which are working across the country. Macfaul criticizes such attempts. He argues that the meet was organized just to send an impression that there is a significant involvement of the civil society in the ongoing democratization process. Since it was a huge gathering no substantial discussion could take place. Similarly, the president came for few hours to speak and left.Along with him most of the senior administrators also left. The meet was attended by the NGO participant. The government machinery participation was for the name sake.

Moreover, the NGOs are neither transparent nor accountable in their functioning. . Many of them are considered corrupt. Most of the NGOs exist only on papers. Consequently, people do not have faith in the activities which are being carried out by these institutions. Therefore they have very less influence on the opinion of the masses. This has also prevented them from being an active partner in the ongoing democratization.

Trade Unions in Russia have substantial number of memberships. However, in the age of privatization and a market economy these numbers are going down nowadays. Yet membership is neither voluntary nor meaningful. In general, trade unions are quite weak in Russia. However , they remain an important focus for study because they possess significant level of potential power. Massive strikes could disrupt the economy or destabilize politics. [6] It happened over the issue of pensions and some other demands related to social security payments for the old age people. Even during the winters thousands of people gathered on the roads in Russia, while protesting against the government's policies of reduction in the expenditures on various social services.

Most Russians firmly seem to believe that all trade unions are "sham organizations created solely to make the leadership rich and the average person poor" (Davis 2006: 207). In addition, many Russian trade unions have serious legitimacy problems with their own memberships; over 55 percent of Russians interviewed in one study stated that trade unions could not be trusted at all. They are neither the "transmission belts" for the Communist party nor staunch defendants of the embattled worker. Over 66 percent of Russians interviewed in Gordon's study stated, that unions do not defend the interests of ordinary people (Davis 2006: 207). Even those few unions that do try to defend workers are often blamed when they fail to make workers' lives better or easier.

The trade unions in Russia are not united. They fight one another in numerous ways and in numerous venues, from the State Duma and the

---

[6] It happened over the issue of pensions and some other demands related to social security payments for the old age people. Even during the winters thousands of people gathered on the roads in Russia, while protesting against the government's policies of reduction in the expenditures on various social services.

Tripartite Commission to the International Labor Organization (ILO) and the AFL/CIO. This is fallout of the post-Soviet politics on the trade unions.

Further, the trade unions remain authoritarian in decision making structure, still allow management and regular workers' to belong to the same union, and continue to receive substantial state preference in the Russian system. The Federation of Independent Trade Unions, with its constituent branch unions, remains the single dominant union organization in Russia, though regional affiliates have shown autonomy, and even ignored the federal oganizations at times.

During the Putin era, restrictions on associations grew more acute. In the 1990s, surveillance of private citizens' communication and lives- a hall mark of the Soviet regime- decreased dramatically . But since 2000, the monitoring of those whom officials consider opponents- be they Committee of Soldiers' Mothers -is common place. The nationwide network that fights official mendacity on casualty counts in Chechnya, or opponents of incumbents in regional elections- has returned with a vengeance. Proving such activity is always difficult, but the behaviour of political actors themselves is instructive. As the *Nations in Transit (2003: 51)* report for 2003 notes" "Many environmental and political activists….now eschew e-mail for sensitive communications, associational life is cramped at best." Under such circumstances associational life is cramped at best.

IV

PRESIDENTIALISM IN RUSSIA

In case of societies undergoing transition strong presidential system has been favored. Presidential system favors a more prominent and dominating role for the president unlike parliamentary systems where the parliament is given supreme powers. It has been argued that strong presidentialism leads to a strong, and therefore efficient state. Legislatures are battle fields of politicians and create delays and politicize unnecessary issues. S trong presidency, on the other hand, leads to fast decision-making process.

The 1993 constitution of Russia was the choice of Russian president and was drafted by the team appointed by him. Consequently it came up with a draft favoring a strong presidential system. It is not just the constitution but also the polity which has resulted into emergence of a strong presidential system.

The new constitution provides extraordinary powers in the hands of the Russian president. It declares: "The President of the Russian Federation shall be the guarantor of the Constitution of the Russian Federation and of human and civil rights and freedoms. In accordance with the procedure established by the Constitution of the Russian Federation, he (she) shall adopt measures to protect the sovereignty of the Russian Federation, its independence and State integrity, and shall ensure the coordinated functioning and interaction of State government bodies (Article 80)[7].

The President is given the powers to decide the basic policy guidelines of the country's governance. He is the chief commander of all forces of the Russia federation. Russian president has the power to issue decrees by which it can bypass the parliament's law making powers. It can declare emergency whenever he feels the need. Moreover , the Russian president controls the administrative machinery. He also appoints the regional heads in the federal units. As a result presidency is the most influential institution in the Russian political system.

On the basis of these tendencies the Russian political system is defined as 'super-presidential'. However, there is a clear mismatch between the popularity of various institutions and level of trust amongst the people. This can be seen in context of other institutions as well.

Political parties which are the backbone of any political system enjoy very less trust of the voters. Different studies have investigated the reasons behind the failures of political parties in providing an alternative to the nominee of the president. But after almost two decades Russian political parties have failed in doing so. People rely more on president than on their own Duma representative or on any political party. In the initial years of the functioning of new parliament it was a battle field between the president and the parliament.

---

[7] See the Text of Constitution of the Russian Federation available at http://www.kremlin.ru.

The parliament –which is the representative institution failed in building any positive image of a well functioning institution which is concerned with popular needs. But Remington's extensive study, the first in-depth analysis of post-Soviet Russian parliament, has shown that in spite of continuous confrontation between the two key institutions of political system the Russian parliament did a commendable job.

A major weakness of presidential systems is that they concentrate power in the hands of one person. In the countries under the process of democratization the role of presidency also af fect the future of democracy . Popular perception of democracy in these countries is linked to the popularity of President. His popularity is considered as flourishing of democracy whereas decline in his popularity is interpreted as decline of democracy . This has a strong case in Russian democracy as well. A strong presidency has lead to weakening of other governance institutions.   As Fish ar gues, 'Superpresidentialism enervates state agencies mainly by means of the personalistic, anti-institutional impulse that it builds into political life. If a single actor enjoys, or potentially enjoys mastery, he or she has an incentive to block the formation of foci of organization and influence that can challenge him or her. The ruler may say- and even sincerely believes- that he or she desires stable agencies that operate according to well-established rules. And yet, such entities are in reality a threat to the ruler's supremacy and freedom of action.' (Fish 2005: 237).

Whenever there was a conflict situation between the parliament and president it was always considered as a challenge to the democratization process. Presidents of Russia have preferred to stay away from active party politics. Election of President has been dependent on his own personality and not on his association with any political party   . In fact existence of parties depends on their closeness and relations with the President. Since President enjoys the decision-making power appointment and removal of prime minister and the cabinet, his office is the real policy maker This has reduced influence of the parties on the policy making. Furthermore a strong presidency has promoted corruption and misuse of state machinery by those whom the President supports. Due to these extra-ordinary powers the Russian political system has been defined as 'super-Presidential'. However those who believe that the Russian President has been much more liberal as compared to other post-Communist states prefers to call it a 'semi-Presidential system'.

However the scenario has not changed much. The conflict between the Parliament and presidency or between the executive and legislature is not over yet. These conflicts have negatively affected the governance leading to a weak state. 1993 Constitution gives extra ordinary powers to the President. He may issue a decree in case of need. This power has been used by the Russian President to clearly bypass the legislative law making process. This had also resulted in great political instability many times. Especially during the Yeltsin period clashes were quite common between the legislature and the executive. There were attempts by Parliament to pressurize President on various issues.

A major feature of presidentialism in Russia is the frequent use of president's power to issues decrees. Many studies have tried to show that after Putin's take over use of decrees has gone down. The parliament has been allowed to play its role in the law making process. The decrees were issued only for minor appointments or for other ceremonial functions. Major issues were discussed in the parliament and decisions were taken with the help of the parliamentary consent (Troxel 2003).

However, another study by Oleh Protsyk (2004) shows that in reality major policy issues and decision making takes place with the help of the decree. Besides, he has also shown that a large number of decrees are not published in the newspapers. This is an indication of non-transparency and non-accountability as it does not go through the people nor through the parliament.

V

THE RUSSIAN BUREAUCRACY

Max Weber in his definition of state highlighted bureaucracy as a major organ of the state. Strength and weakness of a state depends on the efficacy of the bureaucratic system. It is so because it carries the responsibility of implementation of government policies and laws. Without appropriate implementation laws are nothing but words on papers. Study of governance remains incomplete without looking into the role which bureaucracy plays in it. In many developing countries bureaucratic structure has a significant role to play in the governance formation and reforms. Though governance reforms itself demands reforms within the bureaucracy but again its implementation depends on the willing cooperation of the bureaucracy.

In the Soviet era bureaucracy was taking care of a number of responsibilities. It was not only an implementation agency but also agency for change and development. However what made it different was its affiliation with the Communist Party of Soviet Union. This resulted in politicization of bureaucracy. Bureaucratic apparatus was also a part of the political system. Gradually this led to emergence of an inefficient bureaucracy which started working for its personal political and other benefits rather than the welfare of the society.

Yeltsin banned any relationship between political parties and the bureaucracy in new Russia in 1991. However , during the market reforms bureaucracy was a major player in implementation of these programs. It tried to derive benefit out of prevailing chaotic situation of the country. Since the senior bureaucrats have all important information about various industries, they made huge money out of the privatization programs. During Yeltsin's period there were no major steps to reform the bureaucracy . However, in order to reduce its powers privatization programs were implemented. The government sector was discouraged, and it was assumed that this will reduce the powers of bureaucracy .

Even after a decade the bureaucratic structure of Russia remains intact. In fact, in terms of numbers it has expanded. If in 1990 the whole Soviet administrative apparatus, including central, regional and local government and the ministries, numbered 662,700, by 2000, the bureaucracy in Russia numbered around one million. This vast bureaucratic structure has been the core of Putin's social base of support but it has also posed a political challenge.

Recognizing this problem, President Putin lambasted Russian bureaucracy that had 'proved ill-prepared for working out and implementing the decisions appropriate to the country' s present needs'. He said: 'The powers of our bureaucracy are still vast. But the number of powers it possesses do not match the quality of government. I have to stress that the source of this is nothing other than the superfluous functions of state government bodies And yet, despite the huge numbers of functionaries, the country has a severe dearth of personnel at every level in all government structures. There is a dearth of modern managers, of efficient people.' [8]

Plans for administrative reforms moved forward very slowly . Reforms were designed to achieve the functional restructuring of state service by reducing the number of state agencies and the size of the bureaucracy . One plan in early 2003 talked of reducing the number of ministries from 24 to 15-17, while the economic development ministry divided the 5,000 functions performed by the state into three categories: setting regulations, applying regulations, and providing state services, and examined those that could be abolished (Sakwa 2004: 95).

Various surveys also show lack of people' s faith in various institutions accept the presidency. This has further strengthened the president' s position in the politics. Putin's popularity ratings were quite high during his tenure as president.

---

[8] BBC Monitoring, 16 May 2003; in *JRL* 7186/1.

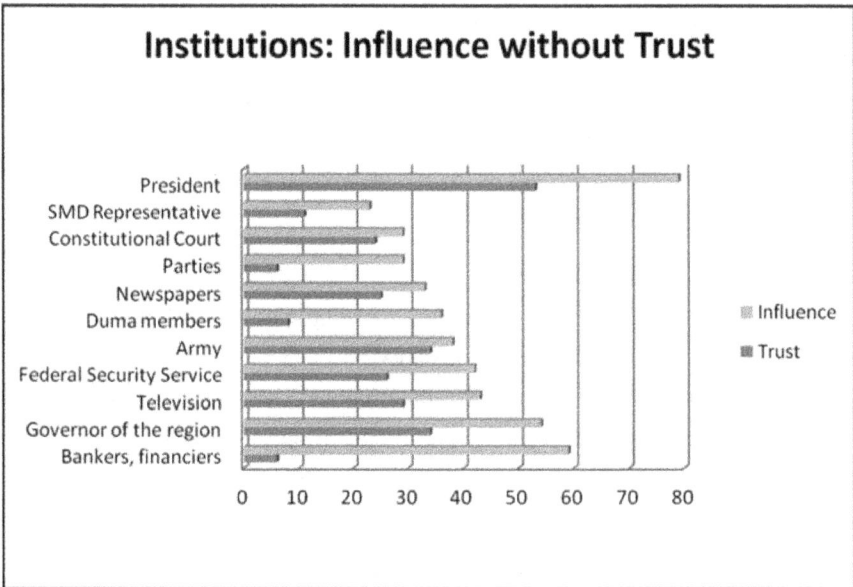

Institutions: Influence without Trust

President
SMD Representative
Constitutional Court
Parties
Newspapers
Duma members
Army
Federal Security Service
Television
Governor of the region
Bankers, financiers

0 10 20 30 40 50 60 70 80

▤ Influence
▥ Trust

Figure 4.2[9]
Institutions: Influence without T rust
Source: Rose and Munro 2003: 226

However, popularity has been misused by the presidential candidates. During Yeltsin's period the parliament was sidelined on most of the important policy matters. Civil society faced regular crackdowns from the authorities especially the media persons.   Another survey of Russian governance in a comparative study has also shown its poor political society score. The political society includes the environment in which various governmental agencies and civil society institutions function. According to the survey Russia scores quite low.

---

[9] The data is taken f rom the New Russia Barometer X. Nation wide Survey, 17 June-3 July 2001. Number of respondents 2000. T rust and influence figur es represent those giving a five to seven on a seven-point scale.

Conclusion

It is clear from the above discussion that the Russian presidency dominates all other political institutions. Such dominance exist to such an extent that Klyamkin and Shevtsova has called it an 'elected monarch'. Though this has provided political and economic stability to Russia but is hampering democratization. A free and democratic polity is yet to evolve. Principles of democratic governance have not received much attention from the policy makers. The institutions like political parties, media, pressure groups and other civil society groups are in a nascent phase. Therefore people do not have channels to express and convey their demands. Consequently   , only a section is snatching away the benefits of growth and a larger section remains aloof from the ongoing transition. This marginalization has further resulted in challenges of governance. Next chapter deals with impacts of reforms in more details.

Chapter Five

The Russian State:
Of the President, By the Nomenklatura, For the
Oligarchy

Unlike popular democracies where the state or political system is of the people, for the people and by the people, in Russia it has not been the case. Rather the state has been working in the hands of the few. As discussed in the previous chapters, the governance has been less participatory . It is centralized in the hands of one institution. As a result, the public policies which are being implemented are largely benefitting a smaller section. This chapter is an attempt to explain how the benefits of transition have not reached to the majority or Russians. The benefits of economic change are limited to some regions of Russia. Both these weaknesses of Russian state have significantly affected the process of democratization.

The governance theory focuses either on the process of policy making and implementation or on the outcomes of such policies. An outcome based analysis is helpful in identifying the problematic spots of policy implementation. This is further useful in developing more specific techniques for resolving these problems. These aspects of governance theory are more useful for the scholars of public administration. They can use governance analysis for resolving various issues of public-policy It helps in identifying various actors which can be part of such processes. This helps the bureaucracy in ensuring a smooth and successful implementation of various public policies.

However, the focus area of governance theory in comparative politics is broader than the theories of public administration and public policy   . The objective of a political scientist is not only to study the administrative and public policy aspect of governance but also to analyze the relationship between the state and society and role of governance in strengthening this relationship. In order to study this relationship the focus is on two aspects of governance: one is participatory and second is its impacts.

This chapter is an attempt to focus on the impacts of governance and state building. The governance approach focuses on the issue whether the state ensures that the benefits reach to the masses or its policies are benefitting one particular section of society. Contemporary governance approaches (See Annexure 1) emphasizes on the issues of human development and human right perspective to study impact of governance on any society . It is argued that governance which produces higher human development results into a more strong state. Such state enjoys more faith of the people.

I

RUSSIA'S SUPER PRESIDENTIALISMAND 'REGIME GOVERNANCE'

On the basis of the concentration of power in the hands of the president Richard Sakwa calls the post-Soviet Russia' s governance as 'regime governance' (Sakwa 1993: 98) and not poplar and constitutional governance. Sakwa writes that "A regime is defined as the network of governing institutions that is broader than the government and reflects formal and informal ways of governing and is usually accompanied by a particular ideologyThe regime in Russia is focused on the presidency but is broader than the post of president itself. It can be seen as a dynamic set of relationship that include the president, the various factions in the presidential administration, the government (the prime minister and the various minister), and the informal links with various powerful oligarchs, regional bosses and other favored insiders.

Most of the western scholars consider constitutional governance as a provider of good governance. If constitutional provisions are followed and the country is governed by rule of law   , it will lead to good governance. However, there are many examples where countries adopted a constitution, which have all liberal-democratic values. However, in practice the politics is not democratic and the state which has emerged in the last two decades is also autocratic in nature.

However, unlike some strong authoritarian regimes like North Korea, Peru or monarchy in Jordan or Morocco etc, where the constitution and other institutions reflect such features, in case of post-Soviet states the regimes have adopted liberal democratic constitutions. However , merely having a constitution does not ensure smooth democratization.

What is more important is implementation of principles of democratic governance in policy making and implementation. Such principles are participation, transparency and accountability Constitutional governance will be good governance only if these principles are followed. In a society undergoing transition adoption of such principles will lead to emergence of the institutions which will work for people' s welfare instead of ensuring benefits of the few.

Such model of governance demands adequate space for peoples' demands and complaints. It endorses the idea of peoples participation at various levels in the process of policy-making and implementation. Besides, in the process of law making the popular governance demands open debates and discussions.

Regime governance on the other hand is guided by the ruling regime. It's the regime, its nature and strength which determine various facets of political and economic reforms of the country. In Russia, since the president enjoys extraordinary power over all other political institutions their role has been marginalized in the whole process of government formation, law making and implementation. Even the media, both print and electronic have been facing cracks downs from the Kremlin.

In case of Russia the president enjoys ultimate law making and policy making powers. Therefore Russia political system is recognized as a 'presidential regime' and not parliamentary In other words it is the presidential regime which determines the governance principles of the country . The parliament and other civil society institutions have either limited or no role to play. Their role and significance is very much related with their relationship with the presidential regime. The paradox of Russian politics during the Yeltsin period was emergence of a strong presidency in a weak state, something that created a whole range of power asymmetries and distortions (Sakwa 2004: 83).

Matthew Shugart and John Carey in their book,   *Presidents and Assemblies: Constitutional Design and Electoral Dynamics,*   define presidentialism as: 'a regime type based on the ideal of maximum separation of powers and exclusive responsibility of the cabinet to the president.   We define premier-responsibility as a type in which the president has certain significant powers, but the cabinet is responsible only to the assembly . The third type is president-parliamentary, a common type with shared -or confused-responsibility over cabinets between president and assembly.'

Two other definitions have been given by Juan Linz' s chapter in *The Failure of Presidential Democracy* and Alfred Stepan and Cindy Skach's article 'Constitutional Frameworks and Democratic Consolidation: Parliamentarianism and Presidentialism'. Linz classifies presidential systems as ones where: (1) both the president, who controls the executive and is elected by the people (or an electoral college elected by the people for that sole purpose), and an elected legislature (unicameral or bicameral) enjoy democratic legitimacy…and, (2) both the president and congress are elected for a fixed term, the president' term, the president's tenure in office is independent of the legislature, and the survival of the legislature is independent of the president…(Mixed systems are defined as having) a president who is elected by the parliament, and a prime minister who needs the confidence of parliament. Other characteristics not always found but often associated with dual executive systems are: the president appoints the prime minister , although he needs the support of the parliament, and the president can dissolve the parliament.'

The super-presidential system of Russia has weakened other institutions especially the parliament. It has also encroached upon the powers of civil society institutions especially the media.A strong presidency has also prevented emergence of parties which evolve out of political movements and struggles. Control of presidency on all government institutions have allowed him to promote patronage politics. Such tendencies have prevented the entry of leaders who are committed to the social cause and not to the presidency. The leaders which are presidential nominees are connectors between the presidency and society but not between the state and the society . In other words, due to a strong presidential regime democracy in Russia has failed to produce leaders who are true representatives of people' s demands.

Besides, with the control over the electoral machinery the presidency has also manipulated election results in its favor . This has strengthened the position of presidential nominees. The leadership which tries to emerge out of society do not have wherewithal to carry forward there struggle. The leaders on the other hand who have the support of presidency also have financial and other support from the bureaucratic machinery of the constituency . As a result, the competitive leaders are not able to have significant impact on the democratization process. This is the reason that so far only the party of presidential support (accept the 1993 and 1995 parliamentary elections) has been the winning party . Other parties have very minor role to play in the governance process of the country .

What has helped in forming the presidential regime is the president' s power to appoint heads of major state departments, institutions and industries. Instead of adopting a transparent and accountable recruitment policy the present Russia government machinery depends on the presidents nomination powers. As discussed earlier , the president has used his decree power to appoint people of his own choice. With using decrees it has been sidelining the parliament which represents people' s voice (Protysk 2004). With this power the president has given benefits to Soviet era bureaucracy and party officials.

On the basis of this Gordan Hahn do not accept change in Russian policy as a true democratic revolution. He says that the collapse of Soviet Union was a 'revolution from above'. Hahn argues that immediately after the collapse the former party officials were given key positions. They were among the key players till the new constitution was established.

II

RUSSIA'S NOMENKLATURA DOMINANCE

In an in-depth analysis of structure of post-Soviet Russian state Gordon Hahn shows that there is not a real political change has taken place. Though the collapse of Soviet state and emergence of a new democratic and liberal Russia was established, at least on papers, but in reality things are not really different. The section which was a significant component of Soviet state structure continues to enjoy its status. In fact in some respects it continues to dominate the new Russian polity, economy and society.

In a fact based analysis Hahn attempts to explain it. He has tried to analyze the data of composition of key governance institutions of Russia: the legislature and executive. He shows that how majority of members of these two branches were associated with some or the other major institution of the Soviet state. They were active members of Soviet nomenklatura (see table 5.1on next page).

Type of post held under Soviet regime	Legislative branch		Executive Branch	Total
	Federation council	State Duma		
Politburo, CC, and CC apparat	2.8% (5)	4.2% (19)	8.6 % (7)	4.4 % (31)
Regional Party	27.1% (48)	13.3 % (60)	4.9 % (4)	15.8 % (112)
Local party	15.3 % (27)	7.1 % (32)	4.9 % (4)	8.9 % (63)
PPO	1.1 % (2)	.9 % (4)	-	.8 % (6)
Party/state, All-Union	.6 % (1)	.4 % (2)	7.4 % (6)	1.3 % (9)
Party/State, Sub-Union	9.0% (16)	3.1 % (14)	2.4 % (2)	4.5 % (32)
Komsomol/ Trade Union	4.5 % (8)	2.7 % (12)	3.7 % (13)	3.2 % (23)
Union government	.6 % (1)	3.3 % (15)	22.2 % (18)	4.8 % (34)
Sub-Union government/Soviet	9.0 %(16)	7.6 % (34)	3.7 % (3)	7.5 % (53)
Military officer	2.3 %(4)	4.4 %(20)	3.7 % (3)	3.8 % (27)
KGB Officer	1.7 %(3)	.4 %(2)	4.9 % (4)	1.3 %(9)
State Industrial/Scientific Enterprise	10.2% (18)	6.2% (28)	4.9 % (4)	7.1 % (50)
SovKhoz/Kolkhoz	2.8 % (5)	3.8 % (17)	1.2 % (1)	3.2 %(23)
Cultural-Ideological Leader	1.1 % (2)	10.7 % (48)	4.9 % (4)	7.6 % (54)
Non-Elite	11.9 % (21)	31.8% (143)	22.2 % (18)	25.7 % (182)
Total	100 % (177)	100 % (450)	100 % (81)	100 % (708)

Table 5.1

The predominance of Former Soviet Party-State Apparatchiki in Post-Soviet Russia's Federal Legislative and Executive Branches, 1996-1999 (Number of Officials in Parentheses)

Source: Hahn (2002: 501)

Explaining this phenomenon Hahn criticizes Russian democrats' claim of revolution. Discarding the 'revolution from above' model he argues that in the new Russia the road to democracy and free markets by way of revolution from above has proven to be problematic. Such revolutions tend to produce "unstable, illiberal democracies and corrupt state capitalist or corporatist economies. Aside from being civilian-led rather than military-led, the illiberal results of revolution from above are evident in Russia" (Hahn 2002: 498).

In her comparative study of four revolutions Trimberger writes that in order to achieve state' s autonomy, "the bureaucratic state apparatus, or a segment of it" must not be recruited from the "dominant class(es) and not from "close personal and economic ties with those classes after their elevation to high office" (Trimberger 1989: 4).

Hahn proves right as an analysis of governance in the post-Soviet Russia reveals that how the state has been facing problems of rampant corruption, capitalist domination and increasing crime. A major reason of such problems has been that the newly emerging political and economic elite have not been provided adequate space in the political system. The existing governance system still prefers the Soviet era bureaucrats, managers and other officials. There is still very less scope for those who come from an ordinary background. Studies also show that the number of people coming from ordinary background has reduced. Only powerful and rich have an access to the political system. Further explaining Russian state's weak autonomy Hahn says that in the post-Soviet period, party and Kosmsomol apparatchiki, middle level government bureaucrats, KGB officials, and industrial managers continued to move into the new Russian regime' s state and business elite.   Yeltsin also built his presidential structure from bodies and personnel taken from the Soviet party and state bodies. A group of specialists from the USSR presidential apparat's defense state security department were incorporated   *en toto* into Yeltsin's presidential administration. Reportedly, former KGB generals make up more than 90 percent of Russia' s Security Council staff.[1]

---

[1] Radio Free Europe/Radio Library: Security Watch, vol. 1, no . 3, August 7 , 2000.

There have been arguments in favor of continuity of old elite in the post-transition period as it provides some sense of stability to the stateA complete break up from the past may lead to anarchy or chaos. Besides, it is also not possible to quickly change the whole existing elite with a new group of people. In case of post-Colonial countries, the newly emerging states continued to depend upon the bureaucratic structures and military institutions which were created during the colonial regime. After the collapse of the Former Soviet Union, Yeltsin also came up with the similar defensive arguments.

However, there is some weight in the argument of continuity and stability but ensuring the domination of previous elite cannot really ensure it. Rather, there has to be a cautious balance between the two. On the one hand there needs to be channels for entry of new sections and elite in the new system. Besides, the elite of previous system also need to be provided some space. A complete domination to the elite of the earlier system will rather create more instability and produce ideological clashes. Similar issue also came up at the time of establishment of the Soviet Union when Lenin also faced this dilemma (Carr 1930). The threat of incorporating the ruling regime officials was that they might not feel comfortable with the new system' s functioning hence may harm the process of building socialism. However , what Lenin could successfully do was to break the dominance of Tsarist era officials and keep his own aides on substantial positions.

This did not happen in case of post-Soviet Russia. Instead of brining new elite in the Soviet nomenklatura was given dominant position. Because Russia's revolution from above was led by party-state elites from the Soviet nomenklatura class, it lacks sufficient state autonomy in deciding its key economic and political affairs. Because many CPSU and Soviet state apparatchiks joined the revolution out of opportunism, the new Russian state lacks the ideological cohesion it needs to make and implement policies effectively.

"This has produced a Russian state with a dearth of autonomy,institutional and ideological cohesion, and capacity" (Hahn 2002: 498). This ideological cohesion also lacks at the level of new institutions. Unconstitutional adoption of new constitution, lack of communication between the executive and legislature, and feeling of opposition being dominant than the responsibility of involving more and more people in the transition has led to creation of a state which still carries the problems of Soviet system instead of a breakup from the past. This has further deprived the post-Soviet Russian state of bureaucratic rationality, institutional cohesion, and state-capacity.

While the old nomenklatura lost its old institutional bases—the party in 1991 and the Soviets in 1993—it did not lose political or economic power , transferring seamlessly through several state reorganizations into the new regime. The nomenklatura's survival was not the result of an apparat *evanche*, a "thermidorian reaction", but of direct recruitment and cooptation by the revolution. "The new regime's cooptation of the ancient regime's bureaucrats and structures consolidated the old elite's hegemony but not monopoly inside the Russian state" (Hahn 2002: 503).   The new regime' s lack of autonomy from Soviet economic interests is the key causal link between the elite nature of revolution from above and the post-takeover recruitment of the ancient regime's bureaucrats, on the one hand, and the post-revolutionary regime' s weak state and political compromises with old economic interests, on the other. With not only the state' s autonomy compromised, but its ideological cohesion fractured, the revolution' s predisposition to compromise with the economic interests of the old *nomenklatura* and its new allies was strengthened.

Richard Sakwa argues that regime politics in Russia is quite complex. On the one hand it is moving forward towards democracy . It is also making attempts for international integration and a less bureaucratized and genuinely market economy . However at the same time Russia' s regime governance have a contemptuous attitude to the citizenry , knee-jerk anti-westernism, pervasive patron-client relations, Byzantine court politics and widespread corruption.

Shelley in his study has given an analysis of elite in the post-Soviet Russia. He divided them into two categories: horizontal and vertical elite. The vertical group is the elite which enjoy full backing of the state machinery   . They also have control over the media, economy and resources. This group is dominant not only in Moscow but also in regions. It has full or partial control over the local media which helps them in maintaining their power status.

The horizontal group on the other hand is less privileged. It is not in dominant position. It has been trying to reassert the role of state in controlling centralization of power in the hands of few . So far this group has not been able to manifest any significant change.   A major reason behind this is the control of vertical elite over the electoral process. This has made difficult to enter into the politics. This group can play a positive role in building a healthy state-society relationship. But the existing political structure does not permit to do so. In another study Olga Kryshtanovskaya and Stephen White (1996) has explained the nature of elite during the Soviet and post-Soviet era. They argue that a continuity do exist between the two elite groups. The only change that happened was that the new elite were younger and more educated than the Soviet era. But they belonged to the Soviet era group. The sectors in which they were appointed might be different in nature than the Soviet era but they belonged to the Soviet *nomenklatura* before. Many of these members inherited and not acquired their politbureau or *nomenklatura* status. However, unlike the Soviet era when it was not possible to join the elite group without being a member of *nomenklatura*, in the post-Soviet Russia this trend started changing gradually. People were accommodated who were not from the Soviet political elite background in various party positions. However, the executive branches were still being dominated by the *nomenklatura* group.

III

THE RUSSIAN OLIGARCHS

A sudden introduction of private-property and opening the market resulted in a chaotic privatization. Due to the concentration of power in the Soviet *nomenklatura* the privatization gave birth to number of oligarchs. Till 2005 all major sectors of economy were controlled by these oligarchs (see table 5.2).

Name of oligarch	Name of business	Main activities of business
Abramovich, Roman	Former head of Sibneft, governor of Chukotka	Energy, politics
Alekperov, Vagit	Lukoil head	Energy
Aven, Petr	Alfa Bank head	Banking
Berezovsky, Boris	AvtoVaz, Sibneft	Car dealership, energy
Chubais, Anatoly	United Energy Systems (UES)	Electricity monopoly
Deripaska, Oleg	Russian Aluminium	Non-Ferrous metals
Fridman, Mikhail	Alfa-Group head	Energy and Metals
Gusinsky, Vladimir	Most group	Media, Banking
Mamut, Alexander	MDM Bank, former head	Banking
Mordashev, Alexei	Severstal	Ferrous metal
Nevzlin, Leonid	Yukos	Energy
Potanin, Vladimir	Interros	Metals
Prokhorov, Mikhail	Norilsk Nickel	Metals
Shvidler, Yevgeny	Sibneft	Energy
Vainstok, Semyon	Transneft head	State pipeline monopoly
Vekselberg, Viktor	TNK	Energy
Yevtushenkov, Vladimir	Sistema head	Communications, finance and services

Table 5.2
Oligarch's monopoly on business

During Yeltsin's presidency most of the state-run companies were sold to the soviet-era bureaucrats who were in dominant positions. Besides, only those who were close to the Yeltsin and his family were given the benefit of insider dealing. In the name of decentralization, enterprises were auctioned at the regional level by local authorities. They were in-charge of the privatization process. In reality the purpose was to ensure maximum benefit for the regional politicians or the bureaucrats. During this trade-off the workers and other social sections were marginalized. Similarly, people living in far out regions could not use their vouchers in auctions in other regions.

During the initial phase of privatization some popular measures such as vouchers schemes for the workers were introduced due to the pressure of the parliament. But there were no attempts to bring transparency in the process. Rather in order to ensure uninterrupted privatization and establishment of market economy Yeltsin made all attempts to by pass the parliament. Consequently, in October 1993, when the Congress of People' s Deputies was threatening to seize control of the State Property Committee and halt privatization altogether Yeltsin dissolved the parliament. Henceforth a new phase of privatization began since there was no power to check. Michael McFaul writes 'When it became clear after the adoption of new constitution that the executive branch will continue with its privatization program, former opponents of the policy , especially directors of lar ge enterprises, rushed to privatize to ensure that they got their piece of the pie before the voucher phase of the privatization program ended in July 1994. By the end of this first phase, more than 100,000 enterprises were privatized' (McFaul 2001: 251).

In the second phase of privatization a new 'loans-for-shares' plan was introduced by the government. With this plan the government banks started providing loans for purchasing shares in the companies which were to be privatized. In one year, the Russian government gave away some of Russia's richest companies. In accordance with this program a small group of Russian banks gave the government loans in return for interim control of shares in dozen major companies. Several of these banks emerged from the loans-for share program with major financial and industrial empires. This method pleased few political groups in Russia. The Communist Party along with the Liberal Democrats severely criticized these schemes. In July 1997 this scheme was stopped by Yeltsin. However, by the time it had already helped many emerging economic tycoons of Russia.

During Putin's period there was a change in economic policy   . Putin adopted a more modest policy of privatization and larger role of the state was recognized in economic development. However, in essence the policies were no different from the Yeltsin period. There were no attempts to bring transparency in economic deals. Like Yeltsin period, only those who were close to the president were given benefits of privatization. In one such case, the biggest sale of Slavneft in late 2002 was accompanied by old claims of insider dealing and favoritism. The earlier director, Mikhail Gutseriev, had been ousted in May 2002 and replaced by a former Sibneft of ficial Yury Sukhanov. Sibneft, under the leadership of the Kremlin family insider and Kasyanov, the prime minister , ally Roman Abramovich, then proceeded to buy up shares in alliance with the   Tyumen Oil Company . In October , the prime minister pushed through the privatization of Slavneft, with all 75 percent of the state's stake to be sold as a single block with a reserve price of $1.3 billion (later raised to $1.7 billion) in the days preceding the auction the competitors, Lukoil and Surgutneftegaz, were encouraged to withdraw their bids while the Chinese National Petroleum Company was barred on a technicality. Sibneft and TNK went on to win the auction as the sole joint bidders for $1.8 billion.

Emergence of these oligarchs was also an important factor in the upcoming political reforms in Russia as they also dominated the political system. As a result phenomenon of centralization of political and economic power in the hands of few emerged. This has led to misuse of power and corruption in various economic activities of the state. During the Yukos affair it was felt that perhaps the state was planning to sideline the oligarchs and a nationalization drive may take off. However, nothing of that sort happened. Despite adverse economic conditions during the recession economy Russian companies continue to play a significant role in the economic development of the country They are major stakeholders in the economic policy making. The present president Medvedev and Prime Minister Putin keeps organizing meetings with them to discuss economic issues.

These economic tycoons have also been source of funding for various candidates and political parties.As a result they also become significant players for policy making and manipulations. They have also helped in creating a legal structure which favors business interests of these tycoons and their companies. This has been a major cause of the federal government loosing huge revenues due to tax theft by many big Russian companies. The Russian government also started adopting policies which favor the foreign investors than the interests of Russian citizens. The Russian tycoons were key players in fixing such deals. For instance Russia's corporate tax continues to remain lowest in the world.

Any change in Russian policy made to attract foreign direct investment not only benefits the foreign companies but the domestic companies also get advantage of such changes. In the last one decade, especially during Putin's presidency many laws were modified for the purpose of promoting market forces in exploiting Russia's natural resources. Ranging from environmental law to property rights Russia is moving towards much more flexible policies. Besides, the Russian companies as well as multinational corporations from other countries are being promoted to invest in Russia' s natural resource based industry (Olcott 2002).

Apart from getting economic benefits Russias economic tycoons, major companies' executives also started taking part in the elections for local executive bodies. In 2001 for example,Yukos vice president Boris Zolotarev was elected as governor of the Evenkia district, Norilsk Nickel general manageAleksander Khloponin was elected governor ofTaimyr autonomous region (Olcott 2002).

The Russian oil and gas companies are no more operating in a small domestic market. Rather some of these companies have got major shares in the world's leading oil companies. Russian oil companies like Gazprom, Lukoil, TNK and Surgutneftegaz etc. Similarly many gas companies are making huge profits out of Russia's world's largest gas stocks. Besides, Russia is amongst world's largest nickel producer, aluminum producer and also has world's 10 percent reserves of the copper. It also has world's largest gold and diamond reserves. These companies are not only significant economic and political actors but some of them have also been associated with many organized crime groups. In fact in the 90' s decade many companies were also in developing security agencies which use to provide security to the elite in Moscow and St. Petersburg. Most of these security agencies later only emerged as economic players as they made lots of money in organized crime as well as security business.

Map 5.1
Source: Martha Brill Olcott 2002: 70

The unequal Russia

There have been two serious implications of these emerging Russian economic tycoons. First, it has created a serious gap between the rich and poor in the last two decades. World Bank analysis shows that a lar ge income of Russia belongs to the upper ten percent and a large population still lives on very less per capita income. A calculation of Gini Index which is considered as the most popular measurement of income disparities shows how Russia is suffering larger income inequalities.

Year	Gini	Reported Gini
1997	34.6	34.60
1997	38.8	38.80
1998	34.6	34.60
1998	37.4	37.40
1994	43.6	43.59
1996	47.8	48.05
1998	48.4	48.72
2002	31.0	31.02

Table 5.3 Inequality in Russia
Source; The World bank

A Texas University Inequality report also shows the emerging trends in the economic inequalities in post-Soviet Russia. The emerging income inequalities have resulted into serious regional disparities which has further affected the development of few regions especially the resource rich regions at the cost of others.

Inequality Trends in Russia, 1990-2000

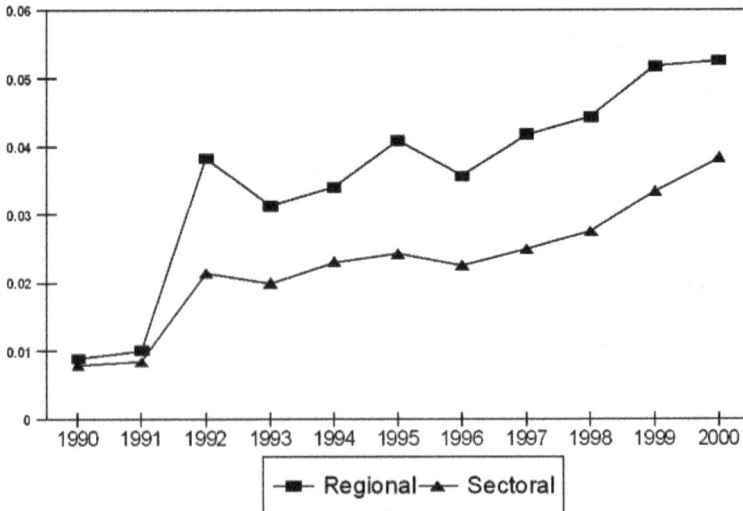

Figure 5.1

Forbes magazine declared in 2004 that after the NewYork City Moscow has the largest number of billionaires. In a popular book Stephen Fortescue (2006) argued that the Russian oligarchs are the engines of Russian economy and not a threat to it. On the other hand Marshall I. Goldman (2008) argues that the Russian oligarchs were posing a serious threat to the state authority. Khodorkovsky posed a serious challenge to the Russian state authority as he started direct negotiations with Chinese authorities for business deals. Putins attempts were to bring them in line with the law of the land. Consequently he was arrested a send to jail. However , this was just an attempt to convey a strong message to emerging tycoons not to consider themselves at par with the state authority. In reality they will continue to play a dominant role among with the Soviet era nomenklatura to decide the fate of economy and politics of Russia.

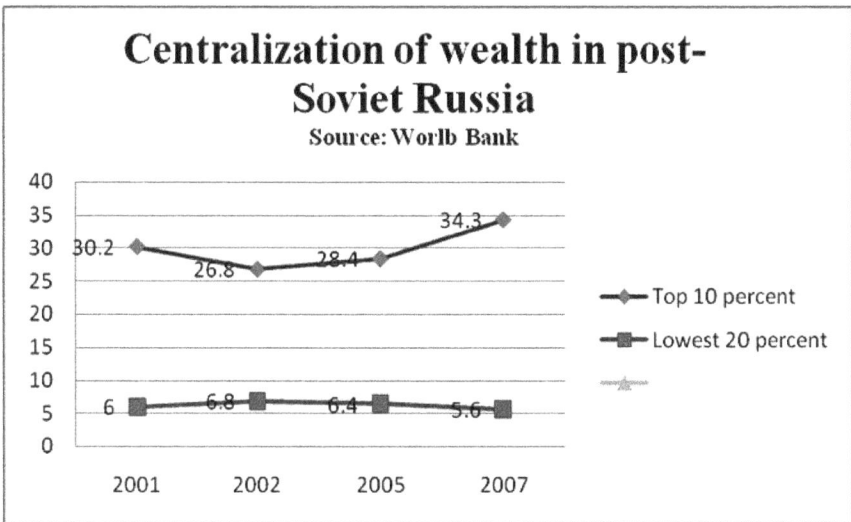

Centralization of wealth in post-Soviet Russia

Source: Worlb Bank

Figure 5.2

The second implication has been the over exploitation of Russia' s rich natural resources in the name of economic growth, development an above all dominance. There have been various reports on the harm which over industrialization is posing to natural beauty of Russia. Many international organizations have also been demanding that blind industrialization should not be followed. There are also demands for a fresh debate on the environmental degradation of the regions of Russia.

However, there seems to be no serious concern for this amongst the Russian authorities. Rather, the activists who have raised voices against this have been beaten up or harassed by criminals as it also harms economic interest of the few . Police machinery also doesn' t show interest in taking such issues seriously. As a result, the forests are being cut at a faster pace in order to construct new highways or industries. Land prices have shoot up in the metropolitans which is giving huge benefits to the real estate sector   . Politicians and industrialists are investing money in the real estate business which is emerging.

As a result of these tendencies the capacity of Russian state to act has declined significantly. As S teven Fish writes "By the end of 1980s, state power in Russia had been reduced to negative power, meaning that the state could prevent things from happening but could not really make things happen. It could harass, obstruct, and repress, but it could not negotiate, entice, or deliver. The combination of intransigence and weakness on the part of the state circumscribed incentives for individuals to participate in the new politics of independent association. It checked the emergence of the institutions of bargaining, balancing, denying, and delivering that normally govern state-society relations" (Fish 2005: 4).

Conclusion

On the basis of above analysis it can be concluded that the Russian state is being governed by a small elite. These elite are not a result of ongoing democratization process but a product of earlier Soviet system. In order to ensure their dominance over the political system and control over the economic resources they have been manipulating the present system of governance. This has increased centralization tendencies. These tendencies exist not only at the political but at the economic level. This has further caused various challenges of governance in post-Soviet Russia. The three major challenges are crime, corruption and inequality . The Russian state, despite having all wherewithals and being a 'strong state' in terms of availability of infrastructure, has not been able to protect the interest of the vulnerable. Only a small section' interests remain protected and preserved. This is the reason that the Russian state is a 'weak state'. In other words the new Russian governance has establishes a state which protects the interests of those who were already strong.

Chapter Six

Outputs of deficit of democratic governance:
A Corrupt and Weak Russian S tate

Study of the creation of the institutions, policy making and implementation do not serve the purpose unless these institutions do not deliver what they are expected to. In comparative politics lot of attention has been paid on the institution making exercise (Pierre and Peters 2008, March and Olson). The outcomes of political change or transition however have not received much attention. This book, along with other procedural and institutional issues of governance focuses on this aspect as well. It shows how in the post-Soviet states, despite the introduction of democracy and multiparty system, the political institutions have failed to prove true on the people' s expectations. Instead of performing welfare, the new institutions are more involved in corruption and developing nexus with the illegal forces.

In the previous chapter we have analyzed how political transition has benefitted a very small section of the society. In this chapter we analyze how the procedures in Russia are unfair and lack any accountability to the people of Russia. The chapter is divided into three parts. The first part deals with the Audit Office of the Russian Federation. The Audit office has not been able to influence and control the corruption practices which are widespread in Russia. Russia is yet not among the popular destination of investors. Its economic structure suffers from the problems of rampant corruption, bureaucratized machinery, delays, poor infrastructure and increasing crimes in the cities. Besides, the reforms have produced larger socio-economic challenges. Second section deals with various welfare policies in Russia have not been able to make any big dif ference in people' s lives. Some major indicators of such problems are the increasing gap between the rich and poor people on the one hand and sections on the other . On the scale of Human Development the post-Russia has not been able to move along with the developed countries of Western Europe (Human Development Report 2010). The social security net has weakened in the last two decades.   Although there have been serious efforts to revive the social security system but due to prevailing corruption and bureaucratic hassle the output of such programs has been quite low   . Health facilities are in great disarray . Privatization of education has led to emergence of education mafia. However instead of development these reforms have increased people's grief. The third section argues that as a result of the political centralization, poor performance on various Human Development Indicators various sections are feeling disadvantaged and getting involved into criminal and anti-state activities. SouthWest Russian regions of Dagestan and Chechnya are the poorest regions with highest number of human casualties (Russian Analytical Digest 2007). In other words, the policy failures are resulting into the crisis of governance. This crisis is different in various regions. In the metropolitans the nature of crime is different from the crime which takes place in the villages or smaller towns.

This chapter deals with the impacts of democratic governance deficit in Russia. The first section deals with the growing problem of corruption. It shows how there are multiple factor leading towards corrupt statehood in Russia. Firstly, largely Russia continues to remain a state dominated and hence bureaucracy controlled economy. Therefore all features of Soviet economy continue to be there. As discussed in the previous chapter this sector works for the protection of smaller elite. This chapter shows how lack of transparent procedures and institutions has resulted into the state capture in the hands of few larger firms in the regions.   Thirdly, this has resulted into various rent seeking policies in the Russian economy . This has a direct impact on the social welfare. Second section shows how the declining focus on social welfare has resulted into growing poverty , unemployment and has serious repercussions on the health of Russian citizens. Finallythe third section shows the cumulative impact of such tendencies has been on the legitimacy and integrity of the post-Soviet Russian state. On the one hand the political institutions are loosing faith of the people. On the other hand there are demands for secession and lack of faith in the political institutions. Besides, violent movements are emerging in various parts of Russia.

I

A STATE DOMINATED ECONOMY

The reform process began with the agenda of radical economic reforms and opening up of economy. However, even after seventeen years of transformation it is still difficult to label Russian economy as a market economy.The economic policies of the state are not in tandem with the requirement for a country to be a true market economy.

The privatization process which was initiated by Yeltsin and continues till today has never been a transparent and accountable af fair. Most of the state-run companies were sold to the soviet-era bureaucrats who were in dominant positions. Besides, only those who were close to theYeltsin and his family were given the benefit of insider dealing. In the name of decentralization, enterprises were auctioned at the regional level by local authorities. They were the in charge of the privatization process. Consequently the pace of privatization between regions was different. Regions adopted different approaches and policies. In reality the purpose was to ensure maximum benefit for the regional politicians or the bureaucrats. During these trade off the workers were marginalized. People living in far out regions could not use their vouchers in auctions in other regions.

Initially under the pressure of the parliament some popular measures such as vouchers schemes for the workers were introduced. In October 1993, the Congress of People's Deputies was threatening to seized control of the State Property Committee and halt privatization altogether . In order to ensure smooth economic reforms, Yeltsin dissolved the parliament. After this a new phase of privatization began since there was not power to check. Michael McFaul writes that 'When it became clear after the adoption of new constitution that the executive branch will continue with its privatization program, former opponents of the policy , especially directors of lar ge enterprises, rushed to privatize to ensure that they got their piece of the pie before the voucher phase of the privatization program ended in July 1994. By the end of this first phase, more than 100,000 enterprises were privatized (McFaul 2001: 251).

A new 'loans-for-shares' plan was introduced by the government. With this plan the government banks started providing loans for purchasing of share in the companies which were to be privatized. In one year, the Russian government gave away some of Russia' s richest companies. In accordance with this program a small group of Russian banks gave the government loans in return for interim control of shares in dozen major companies. Several of these banks emerged from the loans-for-share program with major financial and industrial empires. This method pleased few political groups in Russia. The Communist Party along with the Liberal Democrats severely criticized these schemes. In July 1997 this scheme was stopped by Yeltsin. However, by the time it had already helped many emerging economic tycoons of Russia.

During Putin's period there was a change in economic policy   . Putin adopted a more modest policy of privatization and the role of state was recognized in economic development. However, in essence the policies were not different from the Yeltsin period. There was no transparency in economic deals. Like Yeltsin period only those who were close to the president were given benefits of privatization. In such a case, the biggest sale of Slavneft in late 2002 was accompanied by traditional claims of insider dealing and favoritism. The old director, Mikhail Gutseriev, had been ousted in May 2002 and replaced by a former Sibneft of ficial Yury Sukhanov. Sibneft, under the leadership of the Kremlin family insider and Kasyanov, the prime minister ally Roman Abramovich, then proceeded to buy up shares in alliance with the Tyumen Oil Company . In October , the prime minister pushed through the privatization of Slavneft, with all 75 percent of the state's stake to be sold as a single block with a reserve price of $1.3 billion (later raised to $1.7 billion) in the days preceding the auction the competitors, Lukoil and Surgutneftegaz, were encouraged to withdraw their bids while the Chinese National Petroleum Company was barred on a technicality. Sibneft and TNK went on to win the auction as the sole joint bidders for $1.8 billion.

Fish explains that the kind of deregulated economic system which the shock therapists wanted to establish never took off. He writes that 'The Russian business throughout the 1990s and early 2000s were among the most highly – regulated – in the world. The unwieldy and irrational tax system ensured that harassment by tax inspectors would be an institutionalized part of doing business. Constant inspections by bribe seeking police and by officials from agencies of public health and sanitation, energy consumption, fire inspection, licensing and certification and sundry other agencies are regular phenomena' (Fish 2003: 165). Even after a decade of reforms the economic affairs are largely regulated or rather misused by the bureaucracy .

Richard Sakwa writes that fundamentally the Russian economy remains bureaucratized. At least 10,000 enterprises are still under the state control and run by the state. although three quarters of the Russian economy had been privatized, but at least the remaining three quarters are still being regulated and controlled by the state. In these sectors the bureaucracy has a major role to play.

Growing corruption and wealth centralization

Corruption has been a major problem in the post-Soviet Russia. Compared to other posts-Soviet countries of Eastern Europe which are undergoing transition, problem of corruption is much more serious in Russia.   According to the Transparency International Corruption Index Russia' s performance on the corruption index has been extremely poor The report says that in Russia high ranking politicians to the small level clerks are involved in taking bribe for small work to billion dollars business deals (See table 6.1). Compared to many other countries of the world, including its neighbor   , 51 percent respondents believe that they have to pay bribe in order to speed up quite ordinary works like getting a landline connection, or getting a ticket booked and so on.

Country	Bribery to high-ranking politicians	Bribery to low level public officials to "speed things up"
Russia	51%	50%
Mexico	31%	32%
Singapore	10%	11%
China	24%	28 %

Table 6.1

Source: Transparency International Bribe Payers Index, 2008

Although President Dmetri Medvedev has announced anti-corruption drive as his main agenda but nothing seems to be bringing change in the scenario. In fact what can make the scenario worst is the present global economic crisis which is hitting the Russian economy hard. Howeverinclusion of economic policy making is not based on the assertion that it leads to smooth democratization. Rather it is argued that a participatory and efficient economic policy would lead to an efficient state. A stronger role of state is also favored as an economic policy guided by the private actors lead to an economic society in which resources will be concentrated in the hands of few   . A redistribution economic policy guided by the state will produce better economic governance as compare a fully open economic system with larger role for private economic players.[1]

Income share held	2001	2002	2005	2007
Top 10 percent	30.2	26.8	28.4	34.3
Lowest 20 percent	6.0	6.8	6.4	5.6

Table 6.2

Income inequality in post-Soviet Russia

Source: World bank Data

---

[1] For more details on various problems of studying governance with rule-based governance and outcome based governance see Kaufmann, Daniel, Aart Kraay, and Massimo Mastruzzi (2007a). "The W orldwide Governance I ndicators Project: Answering the Critics" . World Bank Policy Research Department Working Paper N. 4129.

Financial Auditing and taxation in Russia: Lack of accountability and transparency

According to the Index for Economic Freedom which is being published by the Wall Street Journal and Heritage Foundation, Russia is 143ʳ freest economy in the world. Besides, Russia ranks 146 ᵗʰ of 180 countries ranking by the transparency international list despite an anti corruption drive by President Medvedevin which a council was established in Spring 2008 and the anti corruption legislation which came up in December 2008. In Pricewater House' Economic Crime Index Russia stands last as more than 70 percent respondents said that they have faced some kind or the other economic crime and bribery

Transparency of the financial statements of the companies in Russia has been a big problem for the investors. There are major controversies involved with the Russia's auditing system. While investing Foreign companies look for international norms which are being set for auditing for the companies. In the past few years there have been controversies regarding the auditing of the Russian oil and gas firms which have emerged as big players in the international market. Although the Russian government has been claiming that it has been following the International Standards of Auditing (ISA) but in reality it has not been able to implement these standards. There has been a pervasive culture of not disclosing the financial transactions in the annual statements. Money laundering is a regular phenomenon in the Russian companies.

Besides, western audit firms have also come under question due to their auditing of many Russian companies. For example, the auditing of Gazprom, the Russian government oil company' s auditing has come under criticisms from PricewaterHouseCooper's auditing. The fact came up during the auditing that the company employees were making money at the expense of money invested by the share holders. As a result the government has decided to take this task back from PWC (Preobragenskaya and McGee 2003).

Many companies are also not in favor of adoption of international standards as it prevents them from hiding any information related to their trade, business and income. In that case they have to pay heavy taxes on such transactions which they are not willing to pay. This is despite the fact when Russia has the lowest corporate tax rate in the world.

Another problem of institutionalization in Russia has been a weakAudit office. It was only in 1995 that theAudit Chamber of Russian Federation was created with a law . Since the government sector has a major role in the Russian economy, a control and check on their monetary activities was essential. The actions of the   Account Chamber are crucial in making the public sector units accountable and transparent.

However, despite having such a crucial role in the governance the constitutional role in terms of autonomy to function is not clear . There is no clear separation of power between internal and external audit bodies. The Chairman is appointed by the State Duma for a period of six years on the proposal of the President of the Russian Federation. The resolution on the appointment of the Chairman is adopted by the State Duma by a majority vote. The Deputy Chairman is appointed by the Federal Council for a period of six years on the proposal of the President of the Russian Federation. The resolution on the appointment of the Deputy Chairman is adopted by a majority vote of the members of the Federal Council. There is a need to strengthen the office as there is no separate budget allocation for the duties of the office. Similarly, there is a communication gap between the Ministry of Finance which keeps the records of the government undertakings and theAudit office. At times the office finds it difficult to gather the required information. Besides the reports and recommendations of the   Audit Office are not manadatory . They are studied by the Federation Council and the State Duma and they decide the next course of action. Consequently , the chamber doesn't have a say in the making budgetary procedures, use of the public money or public organizations as accountable and transparent.

This also leads to the problem of declining tax revenues in Russia after the collapse of the Soviet Union. One major problem has been the policy related instabilities as the policies as well as the rates of taxes have changed quite often. The Russian tax collectors are more like mafia-dons and political agents. They are also infamous for their methods of collection 'which includes machine guns, baseball bats and ski masks' (Anon 2001 as quoted in Preobragenskaya and McGee 2003). Only in the recent past things have improved due to number of tax reforms introduced by former President Putin.

Revenue % of GDP

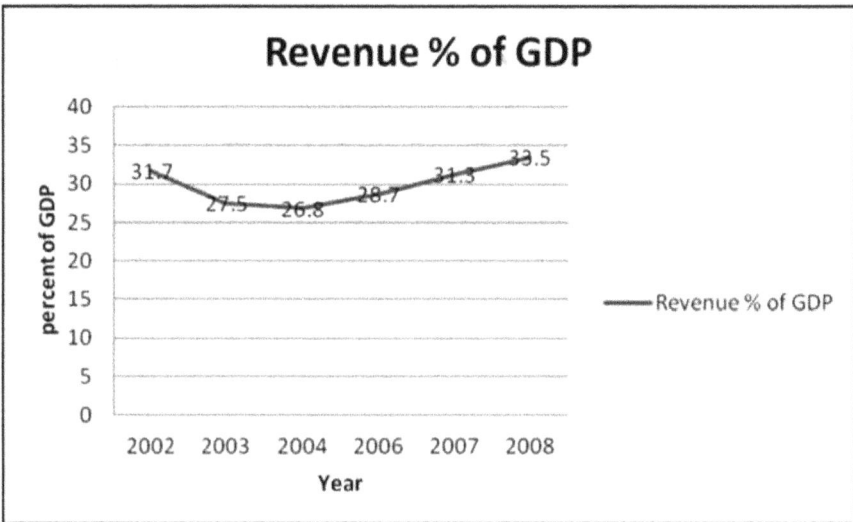

Figure 6.1: Russia's revenue generation
Source: World Bank

The weak accountability mechanisms have also led to emergence of a nexus between the private firms and political groups. In the initial years of transition, decentralization took place and many powers were given to the federal units. In order to make more benefits and exploit the vast treasure of natural resources from the regions of Russia, the larger firms established connections with various regional political groups or leaders who were in powerful positions in the regions. Consequently these firms were provided preferential treatment over other firms.

Though there are scholars like Louise Shelley who argue that the pervasive corruption and the rise and penetration of organized crime into the state and the economy cannot be explained solely by the failure to create institutions and the norms. They argue that he answer should be sought into in the legacy of the Soviet system and the flawed process of transition (Shelley 2000: 92-112). He identifies the division of state property in the post-Soviet Russia as chief cause of exacerbating corruption. He further says that "T o place this phenomenal redistribution of property in perspective, the equality achieved after seventy years of Soviet rule was eradicated within a few years of its collapse".

In an article Slinko *et al (2004)* explain how economic interest groups has captured the state power in Russia and they have an influential role in policy making. They provide few examples of various larger firms being given preferential treatments by the regional governments. Some of those examples are quoted here. In 1998, theVolgograd regional legislature adopted the law "On a special economic zone on the territory of   Volgograd Tractor Plant (VTP)." The law relieves all firms of paying regional and local taxes for the period of ten years if these firms operate on the territory of VTP and at least 30% of their assets are in   VTP's ownership. In Adygeya Republic in 1999 a law was enacted "On preferential tax treatment of the meat-packing plant Li-Chet-Nekul." The law grants this plant a property tax break for a period of two years. The budget law of Kamchatskaya Oblast of 2001 contained a special budgetary item called "support of fishing industries." It postulated that only one firm, named Akros, receive a large sum of money. There were many fishing firms in Kamchatskaya Oblast at that time, but no other firm was mentioned in the budget law.

Rent seeking tendencies

What can be the ef fect of such wealth concentration?   According to Olson (1982) the domination of certain special interest may be a determinant to economic growth because rent seeking behavior distracts resources from being invested in productive work. Such tendencies are more harmful in case of democracies where populist governments do so at the cost of welfare works.

Such trends are defined as 'rent seeking tendencies.'   [2] In such a state certain firms are provided the benefits or special treatment even at the cost of social welfare. Åslund (2001) argues that the state in Russia is a 'rent-seeking state'. A rent seeking state, as Åslund describes is a state which creates a confusing and complex phenomenon which involved a 'mixture of extreme freedom and severe regulation'. He further argues, 'Most rent seeking states are semi-democratic and might develop true democracy... Although distorted, the rent-seeking states are still market economies, rents are endangered by the development of a competitive market economy and intense feuding among "oligarchic" groups. Their drawbacks were initially expanding corruption,

rising income differentials and an aggravation in the functioning of the state'
(Åslund 2001: 4).

In case of post-Soviet Russia, few firms were given preferential
treatment. This has a direct impact upon the declining budget allocations for
the social sector. Table 6.2 shows how on the one hand the revenue of Russian
government has grown faster but the expenditure on social sector has not
increased in proportion.

As a result of such tendencies, corruption has become an all entrenched
phenomenon in Russia. Despite various government efforts no results are
visible. Various international agency reports also show this See chart 6.2 and
table 6.2. Besides it has also impacted upon the human development in Russia.
Poverty and unemployment are rising at faster pace in the last two decades.

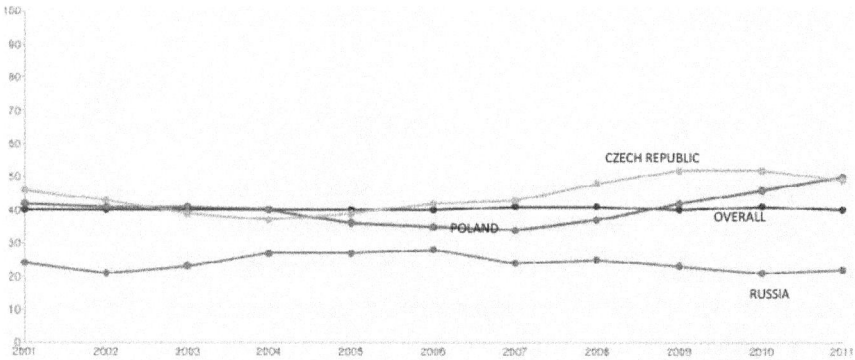

Figure 6.2: Russia's Freedom from Corruption Score
Source: Index of Economic Fr eedom, http://www.heritage.org/index/ranking

Country	Very Ineffective	Ineffective	Neither	Effective	No. of respondents
Russia	29	32	28	7	101
Czech Republic	48	39	10	1	100
India	42	30	20	9	117
Hungary	41	29	16	9	104
Poland	20	34	28	13	

Table 6.3
How would you assess the actions of the government in this country in the fight against corruption?
Source: Transparency International Bribe Payers Index

II

POOR HUMAN DEVELOPMENT IN POST-SOVIET RUSSIA

A major feature of Soviet economy was its success in providing minimum required conditions for a better life. However , due to its overdependence of defense industry and failure in checking the drawbacks of a planned economy it could not survive for long and resulted into the collapse of whole Soviet economic model.

	1997	1998	1999	2000	2001	2002
Education	4.6%	3.6 %	3.0 %	2.8 %	3.1 %	3.9 %
Health	3.5 %	3.4 %	2.9 %	3.2 %	2.9 %	3.2 %
Social Protection	16.0 %	13.3 %	9.7 %	8.9 %	10.9 %	12.6 %
Total (Of 3 sectors)	24.10%	20.30 %	15.60 %	14.50 %	16.90 %	19.70 %

Table 6.4
Enlarged Budget Social Expenditure is Pro-Cyclical, 1997-2002 (% of GDP)

Immediately after the collapse of the Soviet economy and state the social security structure of Russian economy started decaying. Due to the declining state revenues and introduction of structural adjustment programs the new Russian government started cutting down its expenditures on the social security system, such as: pensions, subsidies, unemployment allowances etc. The followers of market economy favor states withdrawal from the social security net. They argue that market mechanisms can better take care of these issues. Aslund argues that in the Soviet economies the problem has not been collapse of the social support systems, but "on the contrary the expansion of the social expenditures to an unsustainable level. In fact various comparative studies of the post-Soviet transition countries reveal the fact that the social transfers have actually increased sharply as a share of GDP in Central Europe, the Baltics and the Slavic states of the former Soviet Union. This trend continued till date.

However in case of Russia things are different. Russian people have suffered in the previous decade due to the decline of social security net.[3] But another significant question here is that how many people were benefited by the social security system during the former Soviet period.   Aslund further argues that "The old social benefits were not very social, because a relatively limited share went to the poorest" (Aslund 2002: 338). He has shown that in Russia, during the Soviet period, only 10 percent of all social transfers go to the poorest 20 percent (see table 4.6). there were number of categorical benefits remained in the books in Russia and Ukraine in 1999, and they were targeted on the old Nomenklatura, which had received such benefits instead of higher salaries. In 1998 the Russian Ministry of Labor and Social Affairs found that 70 percent of all social transfers went to the 30 percent wealthiest households (Misikhina 1999; Dmitriev 1999).

---

[3] During my field trip to Russia I saw people collecting coins outside famous churches. After completion of marriage ceremony the relatives throw coins in the air. The poor especially old people gather outside the church to collect them. Similarly inside and outside the Metro stations begging is very common. for such details see a wonderful travelogue by Andrew Meir (2006).

Poverty in post-Soviet Russia

According to the UNDP reports increase in poverty was one of the adverse consequences of the economic reforms in Russia. It brought with it the problem of low income, high wage differentiation, increase in unemployment level, inability of the social protection system to address all problems, high level of inter regional social and economic inequality . Although the GDP has been growing over the past four years the current levels of GDP/capita and most importantly the Human Development Index, highlighting the social side of growth still put Russia among the medium developed countries.[4]

Russian standards of poverty measurements foresee calculation of the number of people living under the official poverty line, which was around 2.33 USD a day (around 7.07 USD at PPP exchange rate) in the end of 2003. Presently almost 25 % of the population lives below this line, down from 33 % a few years ago.

N.M. Rimashevskaia, in his study on the social and economic impacts of development in Russia has identified three broad features of poverty in Russia based on the analysis of distribution of income (Rimashevskia 1995: 4-51).

A.   The percentage of poor has fallen to a quarter of the total size of the population (36 million);

B.   Half of the country's citizens have incomes lower than $4 per day of $120 per month per capital;

C.   About half are children from poor families;

D.   A stratum has formed that is called the 'new poor   ', representing groups of the population, which, in terms of their level of education, profession, and social status were never previously classified as low income; to a large extent these are the working poor and their earnings are not enough, sometimes even to ensure biological survival, let alone a decent way of life;

---

[4] The latest Global Human Development Report produced by UNDP ranks Russia No 57 in the world with its HDI equaling 0,795 and GDP per capita $8,230 PPP.

E. Two forms of poverty have come into being, 'steady' and 'floating';
    the steady form of poverty reinforces poverty , because people who
    are born into the ranks of the permanently poor remain poor through
    their lives; the second form is encountered much less often, and it
    applies to poor people who make extraordinary efforts to bring
    themselves out of the social vicious circle into which they have fallen;

F. Another problem of poverty in Russia is the ongoing process of
    feminization of poverty, which stems from a complex set of social
    and demographic factors;

The structure of poverty is Russia is determined by these factors:
approximately one third is linked to the low-level of wages and salaries, which
in the case of one-third of all workers are below the subsistence minimum.
The another third is linked to inadequate level of pension payments, which in
the present context (till 2005) is below the subsistence minimum in the case
of one-third of all retired persons; and the rest are people who are called the
traditional poor, which is to say, single mothers with children, families with
many children, handicapped persons and the families of handicapped persons,
and families with unemployed members.

The poor numbered 31.8 million people in 2003, representing 20.4 percent
of Russia's population, according to of ficial estimates. One peculiarity of
Russia's poverty is its spatial heterogeneity: poverty is not concentrated in
any particular part of the country in contrast to what is found in other countries,
most of which have contiguous pockets of poverty .

As many of the poorest regions are sparsely populated, they account for
only a minority among the poorThe southern regions of the Russian Federation
have more than 40 percent of population living below the poverty line in
2002. These regions are Dagestan, Ingushetiya, and Kabardino-Balkariya
Republics in the South. Similarly in the north and east regions like Tuva, Ust-
Ordynskiy, andAginskiy BuriatksiyAutonomous Okrugs in Siberia; and Komi-
Permyatskiy Autonomous Okrug in theVolga also have more than 40 percent
of population below the poverty line.

On the other hand, the regions with a poverty incidence of less than 10
percent are Moscow City , Tula and Belgorod Oblasts in the Center; S   t.

Petersburg City in the Northwest; and Khanty- Mansiyskiy and   Yamalo-
Nenetskiy Autonomous Okrugs in the Urals.

The highest concentration of the poor is observed in the center of
European Russia and the North Caucasus, while many regions in Siberia and
the Far East have relatively fewer people and thus fewer poor individuals.

Such inequalities have resulted in serious social polarization in the new
Russia. As Rimashevskaia (2005: 12) argues, 'There are two Russians in the
same territory, opposite to each otherand differing in terms of their behavior,
orientations, and preferences. The members of "the two Russians" do not
cross paths in their daily lives, and while they seem to be speaking the same
language they do not understand each other very well'. Russia's state-
institutional weakness is most evident in the economic sphere. In seeking to
explain Russia's persistent economic crisis numerous scholars have reached
the conclusion that Russia's economic problems are traceable to a long-standing
neglect of institutional development.

The World Bank report says that half of all households in extreme poverty
were situated in rural areas in 2004, and two thirds of them had children, i.e.
extreme poverty in Russia is concentrated in villages and in families with
children.

The basic infrastructure facilities also vary region wise. The chart shows
the availability of these facilities in Russia as compare to other countries. The
figure below shows how disparities in terms of availability of infrastructure
persist in various regions of Russia. In the regions of quartile 4 infrastructure
facilities are in poor conditions. Further there is a clear rural-urban divide
among various regions.

There is a wide gap between the rural and urban areas. The poverty
rates are higher in the rural areas especially in small and remote towns. Besides
the children, the unemployed, those living in households with primary education
or less, and those living in certain depressed regions of the Federation are
worst affected sections. The World Bank concludes this scenario as follows:

About 30.4 percent of the rural population lived in poverty in 2002, while only 15.7 percent of the urban population was poorLiving in small and remote towns also carries a higher risk of poverty than living in urban areas;

While the national incidence of poverty was 19.6 percent, children younger than 16 years old have a much higher incidence of poverty (26.7 percent).this justifies child welfare projects and supports the targeting of social assistance to targeting of social assistance to families with children;

One out of every three unemployed persons was poor compared to one out of every five persons in the population at large;

Those with primary education were 50 percent more likely to be poor than the general population. The majority of the poor are working families with children, with secondary vocational education, who live in urban areas. About 88 percent of the poor individuals live in households where at least one member works.

About one third of the poor live in household with no children, another third live in household with one child, and the remaining third live in households with two or more children. According to the World Bank a high shares of workers with wages below the official poverty live are concentrated in agriculture, education, culture, health, and other public services.

A major dimension of inequality in endowment with modern housing amenities is between urban (well endowed) households and rural (poorly endowed) households. Chart below shows the poor availability of infrastructure facilities. Facilities such as running water , hot water, sewerage system and telephone facilities are not available to around forty percent people living in the rural areas. Even in urban areas infrastructure is available to only seventy percent of the population.

Problem of unemployment

In the year 2001, 49 percent population (70.9 million) of the country was skilled and capable of working. Of which, 64.7 million were employed in the economy (91.1 percent) and 6.3 million (8.9 percent) did not have a job but actively searching for one. A total of 1.1 million persons, or 17 percent of all the unemployed, were registered with the state unemployment service agencies. Further, a very small number of these were getting unemployment benefits— 1.0 million persons or 15.9 percent.

However, rate of unemployment was quite high in the first decade of the economic transition (World Bank 2007). In 1998 it touched 13.2 %. However by 2002 it declined significantly and came down to 8.6%.

These figures do not explain the real picture of unemployment in contemporary Russia. Real figures of unemployment are expected to be higher than these figures. These figures are based on the number of individuals who officially registered with the Federal Employment Service. Debra Javeline writes that '.most nonworking Russians do not register with the Employment Service, either due to shame or the perceived futility of using the service to search for another job, so true unemployment is higher than the registered statistics reveal' (Javeline 2003: 180).

The problems of unemployment are much deeper than the statistical aspect. Workers frequently work without pay or they work for the pay below the subsistence minimum level. Besides they get temporary laid off, earn money through irregular causal work or self-employment, and engage in subsistence agriculture.

Unemployment rate vary tremendously by region and even between towns and cities within a single region, and in certain Russian regions, unemployment has been devastating. Hardest hit are those cities which have one company economy, which have been producing military-industrial goods that are no longer in demand or textiles that have lost in the competition with cheaper imports. Women and men are equally likely to be unemployed in Russia, largely because women will remain in jobs with the lowest wages and worst working conditions. A large percentage of unemployed are young or pre-retirement or pension age,. Youth unemployment is explained by the 'growing tendency for urban teenagers to live on their wits rather than to look for a job', or by turning to crime. Older Russians have generally been laid off with no chance of landing another job. There is in Russia 'a stagnant pool of the unemployable'. (Javeline 2003: 181)

	2003	2004	2005	2006	2007	4-m2007	4m-2008
Real disposable income growth, %	14.9	9.9	8.8	10.2	10.7	10.0	11.8
Real wage growth, %	10.9	10.6	12.6	13.4	16.2	18.4	13.1
Average monthly wage, USD	179.4	237.2	301.6	394.7	529.0	459.6	649.4
Unemployment	8.6	8.2	7.6	7.1	6.1	7.0	6.6

Table 6.5
Russia: Incomes and Unemployment
Source: World Bank

Most unemployed Russians have relatively high qualifications and skills, making them unsuitable for the few vacancies available that are mostly for unskilled jobs, remedying unemployment has been a low priority for the Russian government, probably because the actual state of affairs is concealed either deliberately or by the confused definition of unemployment.

Nor is employment alleviated by vast unemployment opportunities in the new private sector. Most of these opportunities are available only to residents of Russia's largest cities, and even these are increasingly professionalized and competitive. Moreover, many private sector jobs are casual, providing no job security or social protection, so that it is unclear whether job-makers really enters the ranks of the employed or merely moves from unemployment to the limbo between employment and unemployment. (Jeveline 2003: 181-183). Rimashevskaia in his study has identified five features of unemployment in Russia:

I. The group of unemployed includes young people; men and women of pre-retirement age; persons who have bee discharged from military units; workers in enterprises of military industrial complex; migrants and displaced persons (not including labor migrants); and women with minor children;

II. A steady tendency for 'stagnant' unemployment to spread which able bodied citizens do not have a regular job for more than one year;

III. Unemployment is one major factor in the formation of poverty; one fifth of the poor are defined by this;

IV. A condition of being employed or unemployed differs in substantial ways on the regional aspect and as a function of the specific character of population centers; and

V.   Unemployment in Russia prevails at the same time as an increase in job vacancies, some of which are occupied by Commonwealth of Independent States (CIS) and some of which are left vacant owing to the fact that the persons who would like to take them do not have the professional training that is required Rimashevskaia 2005: 16).

Education

Primary education enrolment has remained around 99%, so the global goal has already been achieved, however reaching a more ambitious goal of 99% coverage with basic education is still ahead, with current average of 90%. Moreover even official statistics show that around 800 000 children are homeless, i.e. unaccounted for and without access of education is not sufficient. Considerable regional differentiation is observed in virtually all indicators of implementation of the basic goals on education. Exclusion remains a major problem, with HIV infected children and children with slight mental of physical disabilities being excluded from mainstream education (UNDP 2007).

Health

During the period of 1993-2002 the infant mortality rate (deaths under 1-year per 1000 live born) went down from 19.9 % to 13.3. However the rate in Russia is 3.5 times higher than the average in the European Union and 1.5 times higher than the average in Europe. The figure for some of the regions is as high as 40 deaths per 1000 live born. The actual infant mortality gap between Russia and developed countries is likely to be even bigger However the World Bank has also questioned the reliability of Russian official figures. It says that "Methodological differences can drive up to a difference of 25 % (under-estimation). Besides regional disparities, official child mortality statistics may be 14-15 % lower than the actual situation, due to inadequate adoption of the WHO recommended infant mortality rating procedure. Under 5 mortality dropped from 23.0 to largely accountable to infectious diseases and trauma/accidents. Deaths in traffic are especially high.

The maternal mortality rate in Russia (31.9 per 100,000 in 2003 against 47.4 in 1990) has been steadily declining but its level remains quite high by Western European standards, which is only about 5 per 100,000 or 6 times less. The high rate is due to some systemic failure, problem in maternity health services, lack of community care and primary health care on the first contact level, and weakness in family planning services. The cause of maternal death in the last 5 years has remained mostly unchanged: ¾ was due to abortion, hemorrhage during pregnancy, delivery and postpartum periods and toxicosis of pregnancy . Abortion as a method of fertility regulation has prevailed since it was legalized in the 1950s.

The health of young people is further threatened by rising rates if substance abuse and the rapid growth of HIV/AIDS and sexually transmitted infections. The rate of adolescent drug abuse has increased tenfold between 1988 and 1999. The incidents of HIV are highest among the 17 to 23 years age group. Poverty, neglect and abuse in families deposit many children into state care of bring them into the street.   About 600,000 Russian children have been institutionalized in orphanages, although most of their parents are alive, yet unable to take care of them. Relying on abortion as a means of birth control jeopardizes women's health and the problems of care for children born to HIV-positive mothers becomes more acute as their increase (UNDP 2007).

Besides, what have worsened the situation in the present day Russia are new challenges before the health system. The health facilities are suffering due to lack of quality and expert support to healthcare, existence of parallel health care facilities and significantly underpaid junior medical staff and doctors, poor material base as well as unofficial (under the table) of official fees that prevent or hamper access of poor people to the essential health services. Family and childcare aimed at quality improvement remain priority areas.

There is a major health gap between the Russian Federation and other G-8 and middle income countries, as evidenced by some statistical analysis of various international groups. Life expectancy at birth at 66 years in Russia lags behind that of Japan by as much as 16 years and the European Union average by 14 years. The leading premature death, ill health and disability , particularly among adults, are; (i) noncommunicable diseases (e.g. attacks, strokes, cancer), and (ii) injuries due to traffic accidents (NCDI).

The government spending on health decreased in the first decade of transition. It continued to decline till 2005. apart from low level of spending, Russian health care expenditure is also poorly allocated and inefficiently administered within regions. A recent IMF study showed that similar health outcomes as in Russia are observed in the countries spending 20-40 % less of health. The IMF study also shows large efficiency differences across regions, suggesting that current outcomes in health could be produced with about two-thirds of the present inputs if the less efficient regions would emulate the more efficient ones.

	2005	2006	2007	2008
Russia	65	67	67	68
Romania	72	73	73	73
Slovak republic	74	75	75	75
Ukraine	68	68	68	68
Germany	79	80	80	80
Poland	75	75	75	76
Czech Republic	76	77	77	77

Table 6.6
Infant Mortality Rate: Russia in Comparison with others

1. High mortality and morbidity among the Russian working age population represent threats to economic and social development and national security. (WB: June 2008: 2 (World Bank Russia Economic Report).

2. Income inequality has resulted into the demographic challenge

3. The demographic problem is intensified due to the poor health infrastructure.

This provided an opportunity to the old Soviet elite to misuse the whole process of reform. It has resulted in birth of new elite which is deeply involved in corruption and male practices.

III

INSTITUTIONS LOOSING FAITH OF PEOPLE

Although there have been serious attempts to improve peoples' faith in various institutions of Russia, due to the lack of participatory mechanisms, transparency in public policies (especially in economic policies) and lack of accountability (power centralization) such efforts have failed by and large. There are empirical observations to show how people have lost their faith in the political institutions, economic structures in the past two decades.

	1994	2000	2004	2005	2008	2008-EU27
Political institutions						
Presidency	18	22	66	58	69	-
Government	10	-	24	22	39	32
Parliament	12	12	11	11	22	34
Parties	6	9	10	10	17	18
Regional govt.	-	-	18	21	25	-
Law enforcement						
Army	41	50	44	43	49	70
Courts	17	19	21	31	35	46
Militia	15	18	15	17	20	63
Civil society/other						
Church	51	-	52	55	58	-
Trade unions	8	21	21	21	29	-
Private firms	12	16	25	22	25	-
State TV	23	-	33	36	40	-
Private TV		-	27	30	32	-
Foreign Experts	13	6	-	-	-	-

Table 6.7
Trust in political and societal institutions
Source: Hutcheson 2010

As the data shows till the end of Putins era people's faith was loosing in various institutions. However various reforms implemented by President Putin have shown positive results. Especially the revival of people' s faith in the courts is the most positive development. However , these turnouts are not indicative of people's faith in political system's efficacy. As compared to the Soviet period vast Russian accepted that they have more opportunities with them (75 percent freedom of speech, 77 percent joining organizations, 72 percent participating in the elections, and so on). However 'greater opportunities were not matched by greater influence." In 2004 the vast majority 60 percent thought that ordinary people have no influence at all on the central government. This figure has gone down slightly but remains significant, 53 percent in 2008 (Hutcheson 2010).

	1990	1994	2001	2004	2008
Very interested	36	4	8	7	5
Quite interested	51	27	40	33	31
Not Interested	13	69	52	60	64
	100	100	100	100	100

Table 6.8
Russian's Interest in Politics
(Source: Hutcheson 2010)

The criminal tendencies: Separatist movements, crime and ethnic crime

Growing disinterest in the politics of the country has resulted into growing social unrest in various forms. Growing separatist tendencies in its North-Caucasus region is the foremost challenge before the authority of the Russian state. These regions have not only been the poorest regions but also most volatile for terrorist activities. Chechnya as a terrorist central point is known world wide. In other troubled areas like Ingushetia, Dagestan, and Kabardino-Balkaria are also under the grip of similar problems.

During the President Yeltsin's initial tenure Moscow adopted a very slow going approach. No harsh actions were taken against the leaders who were demanding more autonomy from the Russian Federation. Since Yeltsin needed the support of the regional leaders against a hostile communist dominated parliament, he even tolerated such tendencies to great extent. Moscow also signed separate Federal Treaties with these federal units.

After Putin became the President in initial years he adopted a very strong and military approach against such forces. After initial success these forces started retaliating in a more aggressive sense. Consequently Putin realized the limitations of such an approach. Henceforth it also started looking for political solutions. Putin made efforts to install someone in the regime in Chechnya who favors him. Consequently a pro-Moscow government was installed under the leadership of Ahmad-Haji Kadyrov. Kadyrov's government has been involved in suppressing media freedom, corrupt practices, and involved in 'Chechenization' in the region (Yarlykapov 2007, Kramer 2007).

	Moscow	Population	Share in Russian GDP	Average monthly income per capita (in USD)
Southern Federal district				
Republic of Adyega	Maykop	0.4	0.1 %	132
Republic of Dagestan	Makhachkala	2.6	0.5	165
Republic of Ingushetia	Magas	0.5	0.04%	85
Republic of Kabardino Balkaria	Nalchik	0.9	0.2	140
Republic of Kalmykia	Elista	0.3	0.1	82
Republic of Karachayevo-Cherkessia	Cherkessak	0.4	0.1	146
Republic of North Ossetia	Vladikavkaz	0.7	0.2%	182
Republic of Chechnya	Grozny	1.2	Na	NA

Table 6.9
Economy of North Caucasus

Russia's non participatory politics, autocratic means adopted by Kremlin, and centralization of economic powers in the hands of few have generated great deal of social unrest. So far in the North Caucasus at least 12,000 Russian soldiers have been killed, more than 80,000 civilians killed and 200,000 have been displaced (Kramer 2007). Besides there are also reports that the threat is fast spreading over to the nearby areas as well. Analysts say that the problem is increasingly becoming complicated as Moscow is more interested in military solution rather than seeking a political solution of the problem (Magomedov 2009) .

Russia's failing economies has even af fected resources earmarked for the military. As Eva Busza in her study shows that low salaries, delayed wages, and lack of food and supplies have led to moonlighting by Russian soldiers, who now act as security guards or even form private security businesses. It is not difficult to imagine entire military units seeking out ways to raise funds on their own. Burza's analysis also reveals a civilian leadership increasingly unable to control soldier behavior (including selling weapons to hostile forces) (Burza 2000: 113-136).

Apart from the separatist movements and terrorist activities, ethnic crime is also increasing in Russia especially in its metro cities. There could be political, economic or social causes behind such crime. However, the fact remains that it is emerging as a big challenge to the security of individual in the Russia.

Conclusion

After the Putin' s presidency there are positive changes in the Russian governance and politics. People have started showing their trust in the institutions. However, the contradictory trends are quite visible.What remains questioned is the sustainability of optimism generated by the leadership instead of growing efficiency of institutions and procedures. People's declining faith in their influence on politics is the prime example of it. It is difficult to predict the future of political change in Russia but it is fore sure that if it has to sustain, people have to understand it and imbibe it.

Conclusion

Lessons for Comparative Politics

In the late 1980s and 90s the academic research in Comparative Politics has seen remarkable changes due to increasing role of non-state actors in the politics of any country. Entry of non-state actors has given new dimensions to policy making, implementation and institution-building process. These actors have also influenced nature of state and government itself. Emergence of idea of 'good governance' and later on 'democratic governance': where state as well as other non-state actors are considered equally significant, is a reflection of these changes.

Another factor that has serious impact on the comparative politics research is the rise and fall of great powers. One such significant case is the collapse of Soviet Union and emergence of a new Russia. Emergence of Russia has posed many new questions before the comparative political scientists. In fact, it has given entirely new dimensions to the studies of democratization, globalization, and economic liberalization.

This study has made an attempt to understand the process of democratization, nature of emerging new political society and state institutions with the help of governance approaches in Russia. Focus of the governance approach was on the procedures of governance, the institution building and their impact on the performance of state, nature of governance and finally on democratization.

In the theoretical section of the study it was argued that efficiency and therefore success of democratization process is not only demands rule of law, constitutional government and free and fair election but also implementation of participation, transparency and accountability.

For democratization, how far the democratic political system helps in the development and empowerment of disadvantaged section of any country is the real litmus test of its success. This can be understood with the help of understanding nature of state i.e. who controls the state, government and its machinery. The study has also pointed out the limitations of existing studies in this regard.

The governance approach helps in understanding some crucial aspects of democratization. It goes beyond the superficial aspects of policy making which emphasizes on the people's participation. Apart from participation of various social sections in policy making, governance approach also focuses on the effectiveness, accountability and transparency in these processes so that everyone gets the knowledge about what is happening inside. This helps in identifying who are the significant players in the policy making and implementation. In addition to the procedures, the governance approach also looks into the popular perceptions about various state institutions. The public image influences democratization. Peoples' faith results into higher participation.

A state supported by effective participation, accountable and transparent policy practices, will be more ef fective in nature. Similarly , a state which enjoys more trust of the people will be more legitimate. A legitimate state is always more efficient than an unpopular and illegitimate state. On the other hand, in the absence of these practices the state will be a tool in the hands of few economically stronger sections. The weaker sections will remain a mean to get votes without having any substantial change in their life styles.

The main findings of this study about Russian state and governance are as follows:

1) The Russian state emerged after 1991 is being governed by a small section of society which includes former party leaders and bureaucrats.

2) The present governance procedures and institutions were constructed by this section to ensure their own political and economic dominance in the emer ging Russian society . This is very much evident in the constitution making procedure. Later on the electoral procedures were also continued the same trend.

3) The governance institutions especially the parliament, media and bureaucracy are also being controlled by this section. President is the leading figure in these control mechanismsA clear nexus is visible between the president, bureaucrats, capitalists and the political leaders.

4) This control has further resulted in centralization of political and economic power despite introduction of a multi party system and relatively free civil society. This has also been a serious obstacle in establishing constitutionalism and rule of law in the new Russia. The constitutional provisions are being violated by various federal units. These problems are more serious in the southern regions of Chechnya, Dagestan and so on.

5) New economy and polity has benefitted a smaller section of the society living in certain regions. A large section remains unaffected by these developments.

6) The spillover effect of these centralization processes is on the legitimacy of various state practices and institutions.   Accept the presidency no other institution enjoys good faith of people.

7) The overall impact of these processes is emergence of a weak Russian state.

8) This has weakened the ongoing process of democratization in the country resulting in higher crimes, murders, poverty, inequality and rampant corruption.

Based on these conclusions about the Russian case some tentative conclusion can be drawn about the interrelationship between governance, nature of state and democratization. Firstly, it can be argued that if principles of democratic governance are followed in the formation of governance principles (formal and informal laws), it is likely to evolve a more efficient and strong state. Such a state will more suitable and favorable for a democratization process. In other words principles of good governance are significant for state and democratization processes. This aspect was ignored during the constitution making process in Russia during the period 1991-93.

Scholars have been arguing that it is the functioning and practices of institutions and not the history of institution-building matters. Here it is argued that history does matter. Though, mistakes committed in the history can be corrected in the due course but a democratic procedures followed during the institution building ensures faster and smooth democratization.

The study clearly shows that how ignorance of principles of good governance has been a prominent feature of the new Russian polity. This has resulted in emergence of a weak state which has further hampered the democratization. Its authority and legitimacy has been challenged at various levels of governance. This has also resulted into the decline of federal revenues further leading to corrupt bureaucracy. Corruption in the state machinery has affected various development programmes initiated by the Russian government or the international agencies. Therefore it can be argued that that a strong and efficient state is a pre-requisite for smooth democratization.

The study has also shown that how a strong economy , bureaucratic set up and police and army might not be helpful in achieving good governance. Implementation of the principles of good governance in all these institutions is essential for achieving good governance and efficient state. This requires a strong political will.

It also denies the arguments which were prominent during the initial phase of reforms that a strong economic system will gradually pave the way for democratization, good governance and a strong state. Neo-liberal scholar argued during the 1990s that a strong economy gradually leads to evolution of a strong state. A developed economy eventually results into emergence of demands or strengthening of democratization process.

The Russian experience exposes problems of such arguments. It shows how denial of participation, absence of transparency and accountability has resulted into the concentration of political and economic power in the hands of few. This centralization has been proved a weakness and not strength of the Russian state. It has also affected the legitimacy, efficiency and strength of state. Further it has hampered the process of democracy building. Therefore the present Russia state in spite of economic revival continues to face challenges at the political level and there are possibilities of continuance of this phenomenon unless the principles of democratic governance are not implemented at various levels of governance.

SELECT BIBLIOGRAPHY

Alfred B. Evans (2006), "Civil Society in the Soviet Union", in   Alfred B. Evans, Jr., Laura A. Henry, and Lisa McIntosh Sundstrom,   *Russian Civil Society: A Critical Assessment,* (New York: M.E. Sharpe): 28-53.

Almond, Gabriel A. and James S. Coleman (1960),*The Politics of Developing Areas* (Princeton NJ: Princeton University Press).

Antony Black (2002), "Concepts of Civil Society in Pre-modern Europe", in Sudipta Kaviraj and Sunil Khilnani (ed.)*Civil Society: History and Possibilities,* (Cambridge: Cambridge University Press): 31-59.

Aslund, Anders (2002), *Building Capitalism,* (Cambridge: Cambridge University Press).

Brainerd, Elizabeth (1998), "W inners and Losers in Russia' s Economic Transition", *The American Economic Review,* 88(5) (December 1998): 1094-1116.

Brovkin, Vladimir (1998), "Fragmentation of Authority and Privatization of the state", *Demokratizskaya,* 6(3) (Summer 1998): 504-517.

Brown, W. (1992), "Finding the Man in the State", *Feminist Studies* 18(1): 7-34.

Chandoke, Neera (2003), *The Conceits of Civil Society ,* (Oxford: Oxford University Press).

Chilkote, Ronald H (1994),*Theories of Comparative Politics- The Search for a Paradigm Reconsidered* (Oxford: Westview Press).

Cohen, J. andA. Arato (1992), *Civil Society and Political Theory*(Cambridge: MIT Press)

Collier, David and Stephen Levitsky (1997), "Democracy with 'Adjectives': Conceptual Innovation in Comparative Research,"*World Politics,* 49(3) (April 1997): 430-451.

Crouch, Colin (2004), "The State and Innovations in the Governance", in Andrew Gamble andTony Wright (eds.), *Restating the State?,* (Massachusetts: Blackwell Publishing Company Ltd.).

Dahl, Robert (2000), "A Democratic Paradox", *Political Science Quarterly,* 115(1) (Spring 2000): 35-40.

———— (1956),*A Preface to Democratic Theory* (Chicago: Chicago University Press).

———— (1971), *Polyarchy,* (London: Yale University Press).

Daniel Kauffmann, Aart Kraay and Mashino Mazztruzi (July 2007)*Governance Matters VI: Aggregate and Individual Governance Indicators,*   The World Bank Policy Paper.

David, Olson and Phillip Norton (1996),*The New Parliaments of Central and Eastern Europe,* (London: Frank Kass).

Davis, Sue (2006), "Russian Trade Unions: Where Are They in the Former Workers' State" in Alfred B. Evans, Jr. Laura A. Henry, and Lisa McIntosh Sundstrom (eds.), *Russian Civil Society: A Critical Assessment,*   (Amonk: M.E. Sharpe).

Desai, Radhika (1994), 'Second Hand Dealers in Ideas: Think Tanks and Thatcherite Hegemony', *New Left Review* 203, pp.27-64.

Dmitriev, Mikhail E. (1999), "Sotsialnaya sfera v usloviyakh finansovogo krizisa: problemy adaptatsii (The Social Sphere during a Financial Crisis: Problems of Adaptation)", *Voprosy ekonomiki,* 71 (2): 53-64.

Dunn, John (2002), "The contemporary political significance of John Locke' conception of civil society", in Sudipta Kaviraj and Sunil Khilnani eds.,*Civil Society: History and Possibilities,* (Cambridge: Cambridge University Press)

Duverger, Maurice (1954), *Political Parties: Their Organization and Activity in the Modern State,* (New York: Wiley)

Easton, David (1957), "An Approach to the Analysis of Political Systems", *World Politics,* 9: 383-400.

Easton, David (1979), *A Framework for Political Analysis,* (Second edition), (Chicago: University of Chicago Press).

Evans, Alfred B. Jr. (2006), "Civil Society in the Soviet Union", in Alfred B. Evans, Jr., Laura A. Henry, and Lisa McIntosh Sundstrom (eds.),   *Russian Civil Society: A Critical Assessment*, (New York: M.E. Sharpe).

Evans, Peter B., Dietrrich Rueschemeyer and Theda Skocpol (1985) (eds.), *Bringing the state Back In*, (Cambridge: Cambridge University Press).

Femina, Joseph (2002), "Civil society and the Marxist Tradition", in Sudipta Kaviraj and Sunil Khilnani ed.,   *Civil Society: History and Possibilities,* (Cambridge: Cambridge University Press)

Feng Yi (2003), *Democracy, Governance, and Economic Performance: Theory and Evidence,* (Cambridge: The MIT Press).

Fish, M. Steven (2005), *Democracy Derailed in Russia: The Failure of Open Politics,* (Cambridge: Cambridge University Press).

Gill, Graeme (1994),   *The Collapse of a Single Party System: The Disintegration of the Communist Party of the Soviet Union*   , (Cambridge: Oxford University Press).

Guhan, S. (1998), "World Bank on Governance: A Critique", *Economic and Political Weekly,* 33:185-190.

Hadenius, Axel (2001), *Institutions and Democratic Citizenship,* (Oxford: Oxford University Press)

Haywood, Andrew (2003), *Politics*, (New Delhi: Palgrave Foundations).

Heleniak, Timothy (2003), "Russia's Demographic Challenges" in Wegren, Stephen K. (ed.), *Russia's Policy Challenges: Security , Stability and Development,* (Armonk: M.E. Sharpe): 200-221.

Heyward, Isham (1995) ed., *Remaking Russia- Voices from Within,* (New York: M.E. Sharpe).

Hoffman, John (2004), *Citizenship beyond the state,* (New Delhi: Sage Publications).

———— (2001), *Gender and Sovereignty,* (Basingstoke: Palgrave).

Hough, Jerry E (1994), "The Russian Elections of 1993: Public   Attitudes Toward Economic Reforms and Democratization",*Post-Soviet Affairs,* 10(1): 1-37.

Howard, Marc Marje (2002), "TheWeakness of Postcommunist Civil Society", *Journal of Democracy,* 13:1, January 2002.

Huntington, Samual P. (1991), "Democracy's Third Wave", *Journal of Democracy,* 2(2) (1991): 12-34.

———— (1991), *The Third Wave Democratization at the End of the 20 Century,* (Norman: University of Oklahoma Press).

————(1968), *Political Order in Changing Societies,* (New Haven: Yale University Press).

Hyden, G and M. Bratton (1992), eds., *Governance and Politics in Africa* (Boulder: Lynne Reinner Publishers).

Hyden, Goran, Julius Court and Kenneth Mease (2005), *Making Sense of Governance: Empirical Evidence from Sixteen Developing Countries,* (New Delhi: Viva Books Pvt. Ltd.)

James Millar, "Creating Perverse Incentives",*Journal of Democracy,* vol. 10, no. 2 (1999):90..

Jayal, Nirja Gopal (1999),*Democracy and the State,*(Delhi: Oxford University Press).

Jayal, Nirja Gopal, (1997), "The Governance Agenda: Making Democratic Development Dispensable", *Economic and Political W eekly*, 32, February 22: 407-412.

Javeline, Debra (2003), "Labor Challenges and the Problem of Quiescence" in Wegren, Stephen K. (ed.), *Russia's Policy Challenges: Security, Stability and Development,* (Armonk: M.E. Sharpe): 179-199.

Jessop, Bob (1990), *State Theory: Putting Capitalist States in their Place* , (Cambridge: Polity Press).

————— (1982), *The Capitalist state: Marxist Theories and Methods* (New York: New York University Press).

Kaviraj, Sudipta and Sunil Khilnani (2002), ed., *Civil Society: History and Possibilities*, (Cambridge: Cambridge University Press)

Khakimov, Rafael (2001) ed., *Federalism in Russia,* (Kazan: John D. and Catherine T. MacArthur Foundation).

Khandwalla, Pradip N. (2001), *State and Governance* (New Delhi: Sage University Press).

Khrushchev, Sergei (2000), "Russia after Yeltsin: A Duel of Oligarchs", *Mediterannian Quarterly,* Summer 2000: 1-29.

Klugmen, Jeni and Jeanine Braithwaite (1998), "Poverty in Russia during the Transition: AnOverview", *The World Bank Research Observer,* February 1998, 13(1): 37-58.

Krasener,————— (1984), "Review Article: Approaches to the state: Alternative Conceptions and Historical Dynamics", *Comparative Politics,* 16(2), January, 223-46.

Krasener, Stephen D. (1978),*Defending the National Interest: Raw Materials Investments and U. S. Foreign Policy*(Princeton: Princeton University Press).

Lane, David (1992) (ed.) , *Russia in Flux: The Political and Social Consewuences of Reform*, (Aldershot: Edward Elgar).

Leftwich, A. (1994), "Governance, the State and the Politics of Development", *Development and Change*, 25: 361-86.

Leys, Colin (1996), *The Rise and Fall of Development Theory* (Bloomington: Indiana University Press)

Lipset, Martin (1960), *Political Man,* (New Jersy: Doubleday)

Locke, J. ([1690] 1965), *Two Treatises of Government,* (New York: New American Library).

Lõwenhardt, John (1998), *Party Politics in Post-Communist Russia* (London: Frank Cass).

MacFaul, Michael (2001), *Russia's Unfinished Revolution* (Ithaca: Cornell University Press).

MacFaul, Michael (2001), *Russia's unfinished Revolution* , (Ithaca: Cornell University Press).

MacFaul, Michael and Nikolai Petrov (2004), "What elections tell us" *Journal of Democracy,* 15(3): 20-31.

MacIntyre, Andrew (2003), *The Power of Institutions: Political Architecture and Governance* (London: Cornell University Press).

March, James and Johan Olson (1984), "The New Institutionalism: Organizational Factors in Political Life", *American Political Science Review,* 78(3): 734-49.

Marsh, Christopher (2003), "The Challenge of Civil Society", in   Wegren, Stephen K. (ed.), *Russia's Policy Challenges: Security , Stability and Development,* (Armonk: M.E. Sharpe): 141-158.

McFaul, Michael (1995), "State Power, Institutional Change, and the Politics of Privatization in Russia", *World Politics,* January 1995, 47(2): 210-243.

———- (2000), "Getting Russia Right", *Foreign Policy,* No 117, (Winter 1999-2000): 58-73.

———— (2005), "Transition from Post communism", *Journal of Democracy,* 16(3), July 2005: 1-15.

Migdal, Joel S. (1988), *Strong Societies and W eak States: State-Society Relations and State Capabilities in the Third World*, (Princeton, NJ: Princeton University Press).

Migdal, Joel S. (2001), *State in Society: Studying How States and Societies Transform and Constitute One Another* (Cambridge: Cambridge University Press).

Miliband, Ralph (1969), *The State in Capitalist Society* (London: Wiedenfeld & Nicolson).

Miller, Jamer R. (1997), ed., *Politics work and Daily Life in the USSR: A Survey of Former Soviet Citizens* (Cambridge: Cambridge University Press).

Mishikhina, S. (1999), "Sotsialnye vyplaty I lgoty v Rossiiskoi Federatsii: raspredelenie po gruppam s razlichnym urovnem dokhoda (Social Benefits in the Russian federation: Distribution according to Income Levels)," *Voprosy ekonomiki,* 71(2): 85-90.

Moser, Robert G. (1998), "The Electoral Ef fects of Presidentialism in Post-Soviet Russia", in John Löwenhardt,*Party Politics in Post-Communist Russia* (London: Frank Cass).

Moses, Joel C. (2003), "Russia's Struggle for Democracy" inWegren, Stephen K. (ed.), *Russia's Policy Challenges: Security , Stability and Development,* (Armonk : M.E. Sharpe).

Nordlinger, Eric A. (1981), *On the Autonomy of the Democratic state,* (Cambridge; Harvard University Press).

Nozick, R. (1974), *Anarchy, State and Utopia*, (New York: Basic Blackwell)

Oates, Sarah (2006), *Media, Civil Society , and the Failur e of the Fourth Estate in Russia,* in Alfred B. Evans, Jr., Laura A. Henry, and Lisa McIntosh Sundstrom (ed), *Russian Civil Society: A Critical Assessment* (New York: M.E. Sharpe).

Pagden, Anthony (1998), "The Genesis of 'Governance' and Enlightenment Conceptions of the Cosmopolitan World Order", *International Social Science Journal,* vol. 50, no. 5-155, March, pp.8-15

Peter Evans, "The Eclipse of the state? Reflecttionson Stateness in an era of globalization", *World Politics* (October 1997): 66.

Pierre, ——————— (2001), *Governance, Politics and the State,* (London: Macmillan Press Limited).

Pierre, John and B. Guy Peters (1998), "Governance without Government: Rethinking Public Administration Theory", *Journal of Public Administration Research and Theory,* 8(2), April, pp. 233-243.

Pierre, John and B. Guy Peters (1998), *Governance, Politics and the State,* ()

Przeworski, Adam (2003), *States and Markets* (Cambridge: Cambridge University Press).

Przeworski, Adam, Michael Alvarez, Jose Antonio Cheibub and Fernando Limongi (1993), "What Makes Democracy Endure?" *Journal of Democracy,* no. 7, 1:39-55.

Putnam, Robert (1993), *Making Democracy Work: Civic Traditions in Modern Italy*, (Princeton NJ: Princeton University Press).

Ramaswamy, Sushila (2003), *Political Theory: Ideas and Concepts,* (New Delhi; Mcmillan).

Remington, Thomas F. (2001), *The Russian Parliament: Institutional Evolution in a Transitional Regime, 1989-99,* (New Haven: Yale University Press).

——————— (2002), "Putin and the Duma", *Post-Soviet Affairs,* (17)4: 285-308.

Rhodes, R.A. W. (1997), *Understanding Governance: Policy Networks, Governance, Reflexivity and Accountability,* (Buckingham: Open University Press)

Rose, Richard and Doh Chull Shin (2001),"Democratization Backwards: The Problems of Third-Wave Democracies", *British Journal of Political Science*, 31: 331-54.

Rose, Richard and Neil Munro (2003), *Elections without Or der: Russia's challene to Vladimir Putin* (Cambridge: Cambridge University Press).

Rose, Richard, Neil Munro and Stephen White (2000), "How Strong is Vladimir Putin's Support?", *Post-Soviet Affairs,* 16(4): 287-312.

Rose, Richard, Neil Munro and Stephen White (2000), "Voting in a Floating Party System: The 1999 Duma Elections", *Europe-Asia Studies,* 53(3): 419-43.

Rosenau, James N. and Cziempel (1992),*Governancee Without Government: Order and Change in World Politics* (Cambridge, Cambridge University press)

Rueschemeyer, Dietrich and Peter B. Evans (1985), "The state and Economic Transformation: Toward an Analysis of the Conditions Underlying Effective Intervention", in Peter B., Evans Dietrrich Rueschemeyer and Theda Skocpol, (eds.), *Bringing the state Back In,* (Cambridge: Cambridge University Press), pp. 45-77.

Sakwa, Richard (1996), *Russian Politics and Society*, (London: Routledge)

————————(2004), *Putin: Russia's Choice*, (London: Routledge).

Schmitter C. Philip (1993), "Reflections on revolutionary and evolutionary transitions: The Russian case in comparative perspectives", inA. Dallin (ed.), *Political Parties in Russia* (Berkley: University of California Press).

Scokpol ————————— (1979), *States and Social Revolutions: A Comparative Analysis of France, Russia and China,* (Cambridge: Cambridge University Press).

Scokpol, Theda (1985), "Bringing the state Back In: Strategies of Analysis in Current Research", in Peter B. Evans, Dietrrich Rueschemeyer and Theda Skocpol (eds.), *Bringing the state Back In* (Cambridge: Cambridge University Press).

Sdasyuk, Garlina (2000), "Russia: Problems of Regional Integration in Transnational Economy", *Social Scientist,* July-August 2000, 28(7/8): 42-52.

Sen, Amartya(1999), *Development as Freedom* (New York; Random House)

Shelley, Louise I. (2003), "The Challenge of Crime and Corruption" in Stphen K. Wegren, ed., *Russia's Policy Challenges: Security , Stability and Development,* (Armonk: M.E. Sharpe): 103-122.

Shelley, Louis I. (1997), "Stealing the Russian State", *Democratizatsiya,* 5(4) (Fall 1997): 482-491.

Shugart, Matthew and John Carey (1992), *Presidents and Assemblies: Constitutional Design and Electoral Dynamics,* (Cambridge: Cambridge University Press).

Slider, Darrell (2003), "Putins Vertical Challenges: Center-Periphery Relations", in Wegren, Stephen K. (ed.), *Russia's Policy Challenges: Security, Stability and Development,* (Armonk: M.E. Sharpe): 123-140.

Sokolowski, Alexander (2001), "Bankrupt Government: Intra-Executive Relations and the Politics of Budgetary Irresponsibility in El' tsin's Russia", *Europe-Asia Studies*, Jun 2001, 53(4): 541-572.

Stepan, Alfred(1978), *The State and Society: Peru in Comparative Perspective* (Princeton: N.J. Princeton University Press)

Stepan, Alfred and Cindy Skach, 'Constitutional Frameworks and Democratic Consolidation: Parliamentarism versus Presidentialism', *World Politics* (October 1993): 1-22.

Stoker, Gary, 'Governance asTheory: Five propositions', *International Social Science Journal,* vol. 50, no. 5-155, March 1998, pp. 17-28

Teplova, Tatyana (2007), "Welfare S tate Transformation, Childcare, and Women's Work in Russia", Fall 2007: 284-322.

The World Bank (2005), *Russia Economic Report (No 15),* (Washington DC: World Bank).

Treisman, Daniel (1998), "Dollars and Democratization: The Role and Power of Money in Russia's Transitional Elections", *Comparative Politics,* October 1998, 31(1):1-21.

Trimberger, Ellen Key (1978),*Revolution From Above: Military Bureaucrats and Development in Japan, Turkey, Egypt and Peru,* (NJ: Transaction Books).

Troxel, Tiffany A. (2003), *Parliamentary Power in Russia, 1994-2001: President vs Parliament*, (Hampshire: Palgrave Press).

Troxel, Tiffany A. (2003), *Parliamentary Power in Russia, 1994-2001: President vs Parliament* (Hampshire: Palgrave Press).

United Nations Development Program (1997),*Reconceptualizing Governance,* (New York: UNDP).

United Nations Development Program Report (2006), *Issues of Democratic Governance,* UNDP *available at www.undp.org/democraticgovernance/russia.*

Urban, Michael (1994), "December 1993 as a Replication of Late-Soviet Electoral Practices", *Post-Soviet Affairs,* 10(2): 127-158.

Urban, Michael (1994), "December 1993 as a Replication of Late-Soviet Electoral Practices", *Post-Soviet Affairs,* 10(2) (April-June 1994): 49.

Valerie Sperling (2000), ed., *Building the Russian State- Institutional Crisis and the quest for democratic governance,* Westview Press, Colarado.

Wegren, Stephen K. (2003) ed.,*Russia's Policy Challenges: Security Stability and Development,* (Armonk: M.E. Sharpe).

Wegren, Stephen K., Vladimir R. Belen'kiy, and Valeri V. Patsiorkovski (2003), "The Challenge of Rural Revival" inWegren, Stephen K. (ed.),*Russia's Policy Challenges: Security, Stability and Development,* (Armonk: M.E. Sharpe): 222-249.

Wheare, K.C. (1966), *Modern Constitutions* , (Oxford: Oxford University Press).

Whitefield, Stephen and Geoffrey Evans (1994), "The Russian Election of 1993: Public Opinion and the Transition Experience", *Post-Soviet Affairs,* 10(1): 38-60.

Williams, David and Tom Young (1994), "Governance, the World Bank and Liberal Theory", *Political Studies,* XLII: 84-100.

Williamson, Oliver E. (May 1998), "The Institutions of Governance"*American Economic Review*, Vol. 88, No. 8)

Zimmerman, William (1987), "Mobilized Participation and the Nature of the Soviet Dictatorship", in James R. Miller (1997), ed., *Politics work and Daily Life in the USSR: A Survey of Former Soviet Citizen*(Cambridge: Cambridge University Press).

Nations in Transit (2007), *Freedom House Repor t, available at www.freedomhouse.org.*

World Bank (1989), *Sub Saharan Africa: From Crisis to Sustainable Growth,* (Washington: World Bank)

World Bank (1992),*Governance and Development,* (Washington, World Bank).

World Development Report (1997), *State in the Changing World,* (Washington: World Bank).

Freedom House Report (2007),*Muzzling the Media: The Return of Censorship in the Commonwealth of Independent States* , available on www.freedomhouse.org.

Government of India (2001), *Human Development Report,* (Government of India: New Delhi).

Bulk of Russians avoids paying taxes", Radio Free Europe/ Radio Liberty Newsline, 3(138) (July 19, 1999).

www.ingramcontent.com/pod-product-compliance
Lightning Source LLC
Chambersburg PA
CBHW050235270326
41914CB00033BB/1928/J